Praise for *The Coaching Classroom*

"*The Coaching Classroom* is a great read. It motivates you to reflect upon the approach you take as an educator toward students. It also provides meaningful suggestions for how you can improve your connection with students. Melissa's book shows you how impactful these connections can be to motivate and support classroom learning. If you are looking to revitalize your impact as a teacher, you should read this book. Great teaching requires continuous learning, and Melissa does an excellent job creating meaningful learning throughout her book!"

— Brian Weible, DuBois Area High School Principal, DuBois, PA

"The tools, techniques, and strategies Melissa outlines in *The Coaching Classroom* will help new or seasoned teachers achieve their desired outcomes faster. This book is a must read!"

— Sylvester Chisom, CEO of Global CTE Publishing

"Refreshing, realistic, and relatable—the three 'Rs' of *The Coaching Classroom*. As a veteran teacher with experience teaching all ability and grade levels over the last nineteen years, I can honestly say that *The Coaching Classroom* is the perfect book to guide new teachers through the challenging first years of this noble profession. It also serves as a raw reflection over our own past practices and a reminder to veteran teachers of the significance of establishing a positive rapport with and environment for our students to ensure maximum learning potential of all learners."

— Breanne Deeb, Elementary/ Special Education Teacher

"Reading *The Coaching Classroom* made me want to be a student again with a teacher who has the skills and techniques Melissa lays out in this highly useful book. From a parent perspective, this book should be a required resource for teachers in today's classroom."

— Debbie Wirths, community advocate and mother of two

"I am highly impressed with *The Coaching Classroom*. It made me analyze my life both professionally and personally. This book will not only inspire educators but anyone who is looking to make a change in their life. The book addresses the importance of being more positive than negative and the willingness to improve how one presents themselves in order to touch the lives of many."

— Elizabeth Drahushak, DuBois Area High School,
School Counselor and mother of three

"Melissa's philosophy and techniques will bolster new as well as veteran educators' ability to manage their classrooms. When classroom management is focused on relationships and coaching, teachers are able to avoid situations that grow into conflicts with administrators and parents."

— Dawna Vanderpool, National Board-Certified Teacher, ELA/Early Adolescence, PSEA Local President

"In her book, *The Coaching Classroom,* Melissa Mulhollan offers an inspirational approach for teachers, students, and anyone else seeking a meaningful life. Her unique approach to the classroom is an uplifting solution for teachers looking to instill a culture of caring. This book is a stark reminder of how we are all capable of making an indelible impact on others."

— Jim Warwick, Ed.D., Owner/Trainer, S3G.security.com

"As a school superintendent, my mission for the staff is for them to make positive connections with all students. Those positive connections foster greater trust between students and staff resulting in increased achievement, improved attendance, fewer discipline issues, and a safe learning environment. The strategies and techniques Melissa discuses in *The Coaching Classroom* can help educators create a positive school climate."

— Mr. Jeffrey Vizza, Superintendent, Brockway Area School District, Brockway, Pennsylvania

"An excellent resource for educators who want to truly make a difference in the lives of their students. *The Coaching Classroom* walks educators through so many options and techniques to create meaningful discussion, trust, and help them to meet their students where they're at. As a school administrator, I plan to share this book with my educators to increase student performance and to help my staff be more mindful of their own personal health and well-being."

— Gretchen Caruso, President, DuBois Central Catholic School, DuBois, Pennsylvania

"Education is a very fluid profession with changes occurring yearly, monthly, and sometimes daily. These changes often come associated with anxiety and frustration that can spill into the classroom. In *The Coaching Classroom,* Melissa details techniques and strategies that can bring a positive thought process to help keep even veteran teachers centered and create a positive, meaningful, impact on their students."

— Manny Barbazzeni, Punxsutawney Area High School Assistant Principal

THE Coaching CLASSROOM

THE Coaching CLASSROOM

Life Coaching Techniques To Raise Self-Worth and Overall Student Performance

MELISSA MULHOLLAN

Published by Half Century Press, LLC

Disclaimer
The author makes no guarantees concerning the level of success readers may experience by following the advice and strategies contained in this book. Readers accept the risk that results will differ for each individual.

ISBN (paperback): 978-1-7354661-0-1
ISBN (e-book): 978-1-7354661-1-8

Cover and interior design by Christy Collins, Constellation Book Services

Edited by Dawna Vanderpool and Andrea Vanryken

Printed in the United States of America

This book is dedicated to teachers everywhere who work so hard to make a difference.

To those of you who are always looking for new ways
to reach your students—thank you.

To those of you who have smiled when you wanted to cry—thank you.

To those of you who have lost sleep worrying about your
lessons and your students—thank you.

To those of you who have spent your own money to buy supplies,
food, and clothing for your students—thank you.

To those of you who go home emotionally drained after teaching all day
—thank you.

To those of you who think about your students on weekends, holidays
and over the summer and hope they are okay—thank you.

To those of you who have been a student's emergency contact person
—thank you.

To those of you who have been working seven days a week in person
and online during COVID—thank you.

To those of you who read professional literature, attend conferences, and
use online resources to update and improve instruction—thank you.

To those of you who hold leadership positions that shape the direction
of your school's mission—thank you.

To those of you who strive for excellence and never give up—thank you.

To those of you who are underappreciated and overworked—thank you.

To those of you who give your time to help tutor your students during your lunch and after school hours—thank you.

To those of you who remember what it was like to be a kid—thank you.

To those of you who walk a mile in someone else's shoes without judgment —thank you.

To those of you who have been teaching over 35 years and continue to teach even though it means you are actually losing money—thank you.

To those of you who have invested so much time and money in your career and could have been making six figures in another profession, but stayed with teaching because that is your passion—thank you.

To those of you who are willing to try something new, I give you
The Coaching Classroom.

Acknowledgements

I would like to thank my parents, Glen and Carol Thompson, who have waited patiently for me to figure out what they tried to tell me for years. It only took me half a century. Thank you for giving me such a wonderful life, for your love and for your support.

To my husband, Brian, whom I grow closer with each passing year. I have enjoyed growing older with you and look forward to the years to come. Love you!

To my children, Megan and Matthew. You are my greatest accomplishment. If God had come to me and showed me all the children in the world and asked me to choose who I wanted to be my children, I would have chosen you. Love you both so much!

To my mother-in-law, Judy Mulhollan, my sister-in-law, Heather DePaolis, my brother-in-law, Chad DePaolis, and my nephews, Tyler, Adam and Connor DePaolis, thank you for all great family gatherings and memories. You all mean so much to me.

To Sylvester Chisom, who willingly accepted my phone calls, texts and emails and patiently answered all my questions about publishing. Thank you.

To Peggy Caruso, Nikki Iozzo and Debbie Wirths for spending weeks with me going over my rough draft and giving such fantastic suggestions. Thank you, Peggy for teaching me these life coaching techniques and for putting me in touch with so many people in the industry who could walk me through this process. Thank you, Debbie for sticking with me from start to finish.

To Barry Fillman, who has supported this endeavor, provided the information I needed and encouraged me to tell the world what I had put into practice in the classroom.

To Diane Oberlin, a true friend and my co-teacher for ten years. Thank you for letting me bend your ear about everything—including this book. You are a wonderful confidant. You were with me as I implemented all that I have written about in this book. I appreciate your support and feedback.

To Dawna Vanderpool for going over this book, and going over this book and going over this book. You are such an intelligent, reliable person. I appreciate you so much.

Thank you, Pam Kerr, for reminding me to take time for myself during this endeavor. I am so thankful to work alongside of you.

Thank you to Lauren Wingert for all the work you did to help me get started with this book. You are very talented young lady.

Thank you, Mrs. Hankey, Mrs. Shoup (Grzegorzewski) and Mrs. Mook for being English teachers who got me interested in English and inspired me to become an English teacher—not an easy task.

To my students, who have taught me as much as I taught you—thank you.

Thank you to my Maker for giving me the talent to teach, to write and for guiding me on this journey.

A special thank you to Andrea Vanryken for doing such a fantastic job with the final editing of my book, to Jeremy Avenarius for his expertise and help with my website and logo design, to Christy Collins for the phenomenal job on my cover and book design, to Maggie McLaughlin for putting together my ebook and to Martha Bullen, who has walked me through this entire process. Without all of you, I could not have made this book a reality.

Contents

Foreword

When we consider all that students have going on in their lives today, as well as the expectations and responsibilities placed on schools by society, it is staggering.

As a former school administrator and learning skills specialist, I find Melissa Mulhollan's *The Coaching Classroom* refreshing. The positive behavior concept, focusing first on the teacher then modeling those behaviors in the classroom, has great potential to make a difference in a student's life, not only academically, but for a lifetime.

Below are several important aspects of her book that I discovered:

- Individual student needs keep growing and increasing.
- Schools are expected to do more and more for students.
- To make change in someone else, make changes in yourself first.
- Ideas and suggestions to help maintain and stay positive.
- The importance of incorporating positives in everyday life.
- When a teacher models positive behavior, family, friends, colleagues, students, and their parents are affected.
- Build positive relationships inside and outside the classroom.
- Students do not care how much we know until they know how much we care for them.

- Providing a positive and inviting learning environment/climate enhances the academic experience for students.
- Making the classroom learning experience positive and relevant to the student has great impact not only on learning but everyday life as well.
- The success of any classroom is the effect that it has on students.
- Academic grades and standardized test scores are improving significantly.
- *The Coaching Classroom* provides and models ideas and suggestions for colleagues to make positive changes in their classrooms.
- Individual student testimonies acknowledge the impact that *The Coaching Classroom* has had on each one's life.
- *The Coaching Classroom* is for ALL students.
- *The Coaching Classroom* has a positive impact on the entire school at Jeff Tech.

— Dr. Fred Park, Chairperson of the school board of The Jefferson County-DuBois Area Vocational-Technical School (Jeff Tech) in Pennsylvania

Introduction

Life coaching and self-help are all the rage today. And it's no wonder! It is no secret that we need to find positive ways to navigate our world today. Our students are coming to us from backgrounds that make it any wonder they can function at all, let alone achieve success on standardized tests or become college- and career-ready. Between dysfunction in homes and rampant substance abuse, learning about photosynthesis, Charles Dickens, the American Revolution, or slope-intercept is most likely the furthest thing from their minds.

There are not enough hours in the day to teach the material let alone counsel them while they are in class. And that is not our job, right? That is why students have parents, guidance counselors, student assistance teams, and other programs to help with their problems.

In participating in our annual mandatory online training on child abuse, I watched a video during which Dr. Jack P. Shonkoff, MD, from Harvard University talked about our responsibility to the children of the world, and it really struck a chord with me. He said, "Neglecting young children is neglecting the foundations of a healthy next generation. A community pays a huge price later. Whether it is educational achievement, economic productivity, good citizenship, or the ability to parent the next generation. All of the things that have to do with a healthy, prosperous society."

The definition of neglect is quite simply the failure to be cared for properly. Not all neglect is intentional. But it is happening at an alarming rate. In 2018, there were roughly 3,500,000 reports of abuse of children. Sixty-point-eight percent were a result of neglect. More children enter foster care due to neglect than child abuse. We can say that the burden falls on parents and other professionals and not us, but when we consider the detrimental effect such lack of care has on the progress of society, I find it difficult to argue that we do not hold some responsibility in providing whatever care we can demonstrate in our capacity as educators.

The bottom line is that we can offer the best lesson in the world, but if students' minds are not in the right place to receive the information we are attempting to teach them, the students won't learn the material. I hear teachers complain all the time about "these kids." "These kids" are disrespectful, "these kids" are lazy, "these kids" just don't care, "these kids" spend too much time playing video games and on social media, "these kids" _____ (you fill in the blank).

There is no doubt that most of these complaints have merit. The problem is that while we can work to modify unacceptable student behaviors, the truth is we can only change ourselves. That does not mean that students will not benefit from a coaching classroom approach. However, beginning with the idea that we are going to change *someone else* is not the best way to look at *The Coaching Classroom* philosophy.

Instead, we change *ourselves* and then use that change to help others curb negative actions by modeling the behaviors we wish to see. So, by improving ourselves, we deal with students' negative behaviors with a more positive approach.

If "these kids" have all "these issues," the best way to help them, first and foremost, is to help ourselves. In doing so, we can reach them despite the baggage they bring to school every day.

Introduction

Now, I may have started to lose some of you at this point, but please hear me out. I am not suggesting that we make our courses easier or more entertaining. I don't expect us to put couches in our classrooms and allow students to lie down and pour their hearts out to us.

Some educators become upset with the idea that they are expected to change to meet the needs of their students. I hear it all the time. "Why do I have to adapt my expectations to meet the needs of kids who don't care, are strung out on drugs, or are just plain lazy?" That is a fair question. Chapter One will explain why making changes in ourselves is so important to not only our own well-being but the well-being of our students.

Some believe, especially at the secondary level, that we should just let them fail, and then they will learn their lesson. It's their fault, after all. It's almost insulting to ask us to continually make concessions for persons who refuse to do anything to make their own lives any better. I agree. It is very difficult to find the balance between enabling poor behaviors and creating a classroom that supports learning when so many appear disinterested in learning at all.

Here is what I have learned through the implementation of my life coaching techniques in the classroom: These kids feel bad about themselves and their lives already. Allowing them to fail only reinforces their negative beliefs about themselves as well as the people and world around them. We are not showing them anything different than what they already believe in their subconscious minds about what they can accomplish and what they deserve.

Therefore, the lesson we are hoping they learn by allowing them to fail is ineffective. I am certain that, with proper implementation, you will be shocked at the positive effect these coaching techniques will have on "these kids" both in and out of the classroom setting.

The key is to remember that students' beliefs about themselves, others, and the world around them didn't get ingrained in their minds overnight. Recalling information about the developmental stages of youth from that long-ago Psychology 101 course will help us tailor our classroom lessons (and life lessons) to our students. It helps us understand the beliefs and behaviors they bring to the classroom.

If you are like me, even though we know this information already, we must be reminded periodically. It is too easy to fall into the pattern of placing blame and becoming frustrated and defeated by the apathy and poor behaviors exhibited by some of our students instead of remembering why it is happening and finding solutions to help them. Again, adjusting our mindset about their behavior is the only way to curb the behavior.

Remember, I am not suggesting that we forego accountability for their actions. No one is saying that students cannot control themselves, so we should just pacify them. I like to look at it as being tolerant yet still holding them accountable. There is a balancing act that must happen here. We must set a certain standard of expectations while still being approachable.

Those of us who are veteran educators have had the pleasure of being visited years later by former students for the sole purpose of thanking us. We appreciate every visit, of course, but sometimes we are completely surprised, aren't we? Every once in awhile, we realize we made a positive impact on a child even though we had no idea at the time. The truth is we do not always know the effect we have on our students, and we may never know since they do not always come back and tell us. We simply do our best and hope that we are making a difference in their lives.

We must also remember that some students may want to make positive changes, but there are reasons we do not see much progress. Some may not be quite ready for it yet, while others may have been programmed for so long that they will need years of this type of reinforcement to make a change, not to mention the fact that some people may resist us no matter what we do. Some kids will simply put up that wall—those students are not seeking help from us and will not welcome it.

It is truly different coaching people in an office, as clients, as opposed to coaching students in a classroom setting. In the office, clients have come to us seeking assistance. They are paying for our services, and the hour is their time, and theirs alone. In a classroom setting, we are compelling them to use these techniques, and some will simply resist. That's okay.

I do not want you to feel defeated before you even get started, but I also do not want you to believe that I am telling you that 100 percent of my students are receptive and successful with *The Coaching Classroom*. I remember being a new teacher, fresh out of college, who was sold the bill of goods that as long as you have a fantastic, creative lesson and are enthusiastic, your students will be as well. I remember wondering what I was doing wrong over and over again as not all my students were interested in my lessons.

The Coaching Classroom works. It is worth reading this book and implementing the techniques because you will be successful. Success does not require 100 percent buy-in.

Further, you may not know you have reached a student until years down the road. Honestly, it is no different than what happens with our lessons that pertain to the curriculum. We don't quit attempting to teach students the curriculum when one of our lessons isn't received the way we thought it would. The same holds true with *The Coaching Classroom* techniques.

We know we cannot save them all, and even if we make progress one year, we may watch them slide backward the next if their teachers do not put these techniques into practice. Students will have setbacks, and they will falter. After all, the hardest thing in the world to change is who we are. That fact is particularly true if we do not see that our behaviors are serving our best interests.

Even when we want to make positive changes, we often fall short. How many times do people set out to eat right and exercise only to fall right back into bad eating habits and a more sedentary lifestyle? We can simply look at the number of people who make New Year's resolutions and actually maintain those changes to know the truth of this statement. We *know better* and yet we often crash and burn.

However, there are a few things to remember when considering using this approach in our classrooms.

1. Reaching one student is better than reaching none at all.

2. Even if students do not use the tools right now, someday they may recall them and use them.

3. It cannot hurt to bring more positivity into the classroom setting. As a matter of fact, in this world, it may be a welcome change.

After twenty-nine years in the classroom and twenty-three spent raising my own children, I know that there is no one solution that works for everyone. We are all coming to the job with a variety of situations that will, without a doubt, impact how we implement the techniques of *The Coaching Classroom*. Even our personalities and comfort levels will affect how we use these techniques. That is why Chapter Two has been dedicated to helping you find ways to stay positive, even if your space at home or work is negative. Being in a positive mindset when occupying those spaces can be more challenging, but you will see it is not impossible.

Because my work environment has been in settings teaching grades 9 through 12, this guide may seem geared more toward middle-school and high-school instructors. However, almost every single idea I present in this book can be tailored to any grade level and used by anyone who wants to make positive changes in themselves that will influence those around them. Chapter Three will even share with you how you can use these techniques without disrupting the ability to get through your curriculum.

So, while this book is written to assist anyone in education, it can be used and incorporated by everyone, especially those who have influence over children—parents, coaches, Sunday school teachers, health care professionals specializing in pediatrics, and so forth.

We are all works in progress that must continuously be tweaked throughout our lives as we grow and change. I am always working on myself to be a better person, teacher, wife, mother, friend...and I plan to work on myself for the rest of my life. If you ask anyone to tell you something about themselves that they should change, most people would be able to answer that question easily. Identifying what needs changing is often the simple part. The difficulty is figuring out how to make that change. Chapter Four is dedicated to teaching you how to make changes to remove what no longer works for you. Then, once you make changes in yourself, you will want to begin implementing coaching techniques in your classroom setting. Chapter Five will give you ideas about how to use the techniques you implemented to make changes in yourself with your students in the classroom setting.

When we think we have reached a pinnacle and do not need to do any more work to be the best we can be, we are sadly mistaken. I believe life consists of one lesson after another. We can take those lessons and ignore them, or we can use them to our advantage. I prefer the latter. The best way to keep these lessons flowing is to incorporate them into all aspects of your life. Once you have used them for self-improvement and in the classroom, you can then find ideas in Chapter Six on how to incorporate them with your family and friends. We all know that the more we use a skill, the more practiced we become at it. Chapter Six gives you ideas on how to use coaching classroom techniques outside of yourself and your work environment.

Rest assured that you do not have to become a certified life coach to use these techniques in your classroom. I will share with you all that you need to know to effectively utilize coaching techniques in your classroom setting. You could still take a life coaching course and become a certified life coach if you wish. In doing so, it will help you become a better person and therefore a better instructor. However, I just want to be clear that it is not a prerequisite to creating a coaching classroom.

The only prerequisite for improving ourselves, and therefore our classrooms, is the desire to do so. You may try it for a while and then feel yourself sliding back into old habits. That is your own subconscious mind and the behaviors that were modeled for you bringing you back to your comfort zone. Most of us are always looking for fresh ideas for ways to improve what we do in the classroom. Chapter Seven provides some of the tools needed to add new and exciting life coaching techniques into your classroom.

At that point, you may need to revisit this book to become inspired again. Sometimes we become complacent and begin to slide back into our old ways because they were comfortable and easier. One of the reasons it becomes easier to slide back into old habits is because when we are happy and succeeding, we find that not everyone in our lives shares in our joy about the positive changes we make in ourselves, our job setting, and our personal lives. Chapter Eight will teach us how to handle those naysayers and keep moving forward instead of sliding backward.

Complacency and ease are not the only reasons we regress. Our jobs are a challenge on the best days. I still have bad days both in and out of the work setting. So, even though I wrote this book/guide, I also need to find ways to persevere and get myself fired up again and again.

A few years ago, I had a group of thirty-two students during the last period of the day. The majority of the students had challenging personalities and a vast array of emotional needs. The negative energy during that eighty-minute period, along with the effort so many would expend *trying* to be unsuccessful (like it was a badge of honor!), easily wore me down. I had to put into practice numerous life coaching techniques from my daily repertoire to get myself in the right frame of mind to manage that group successfully each day. If I hadn't, I don't think I could have managed that group without doing an injustice to myself and ultimately to them.

Introduction

Now more than ever, we need life coaching techniques for ourselves and our students. When schools closed in March of 2020 and did not reopen for the remainder of the 2019-2020 school year, we realized that we had new territory, uncharted ground that we would be covering.

Taking care of ourselves, physically as well as mentally, is crucial now more than ever. As we tend to the multifaceted needs of our students, we are realizing, maybe for the first time for some of us, how far our role extends into their lives. Virtual learning has forced us to begin a new way of inspiring our students to find success, and a host of new obstacles stand in our way.

We know that for some of our students, being at home 24/7 during this time has exacerbated the emotional and physical turmoil of their lives. Fabulous lessons teaching the approved curriculum are certainly noteworthy, but some students need more than creative lessons.

I have seen many school personnel go above and beyond with their lessons during this time. But I also know that many teachers have faced stressors in addition to financial and social, for example, constantly juggling the roles of parent, home-school instructor, and virtual educator. We need to get in the right mindset so we can help ourselves, our families, and our students.

No matter how you navigated through this unprecedented time in our lives, we have completed the remainder of this school year unsure of the future, waiting for decisions to be made as to how the new school year will look. As we return, the question remains if we will stay in session or end up teaching virtually once more.

Whether we continue on the path of virtual instruction, use a staggered schedule enforcing social distancing and limiting class size, or miraculously return to business as usual and remain in session for the rest of the school year, creating space for positivity in our lessons is imperative. Everything I present in this book can work with virtual or real-time instruction.

Like I said, we are all works in progress. Changing our perspectives and abandoning a teaching style that is unfamiliar to us can seem risky at best and terrifying at worst. Rising above the challenges we face as educators can be grueling. But as lifelong learners who strive for our own personal best to help our students thrive, incorporating *The Coaching Classroom* personally and professionally is a step in the right direction. If all my anecdotes don't convince you, then Chapter Nine will provide the data and testimonials you may need to decide to put *The Coaching Classroom* to use in your life and career.

CHAPTER 1

How to Have a Bad Day

*Coping Strategies to Conquer Rough Days While
Still Modeling Positive Behavior for Others*

We are all human, and we all have bad days. When I first became a life coach I was shocked by the number of people who expected me to be in a great mood all the time. Life Coaches have bad days too. Life Coaches cry and get upset and angry. Life Coaches are human. And yet, when I would have a moment, life coaching would get thrown in my face with comments like, "I thought you were supposed to be Miss Positivity?" or, "That comment doesn't sound very *positive.*"

Here is the truth of the matter—life coaching won't make us perfect, but it does help us choose to respond in place of reacting to situations. It also teaches us how to let go of a mood that is not serving our best interest more quickly than the average person. But know this: I have had bad days in my classroom and even in my personal life, days during which I wish I could have a do-over.

The key is learning from it, figuring out where it came from, resolving to find a way to make sure that it won't happen again, forgiving ourselves and/or others, and then learning to let it go. We must allow ourselves to be human and then allow our students to be human too. When we do, we will not be letting ourselves down when we make a mistake, and we will be more tolerant of our students' idiosyncrasies as well.

It is imperative to acknowledge and accept where the behavior is coming from while at the same time making students understand that they are still accountable for their unacceptable actions. That task is much easier when we exhibit compassion and understanding toward a student in place of frustration and disgust. Our demeanor, therefore, plays a huge role in helping students accept consequences for their actions in lieu of rebelling against the consequences or simply making excuses for the poor behaviors.

To aid us in being more compassionate and understanding, let's review how the mind works. From birth to age seven, our students develop their views of the world: their subconscious minds. This stage of development is when we form our opinions of the world. This is the part of the mind that, in essence, rules our behaviors. Did you ever respond to a situation in a way that surprised you? Most likely, that response had to do with something that was ingrained in your subconscious mind. Your subconscious mind is the gateway to understanding why you do what you do even when you know better.

The next stage occurs between ages seven and fourteen. During this stage of development, students begin to model the behaviors they see in their family and friends, on TV, in the movies, from social media, and even from video games. They can elect to model the behaviors of teachers as well. Knowing that they may model their behavior on ours at this stage should make us even more concerned about how we interact with them.

The last stage occurs from age fourteen to twenty-one, when students take what is ingrained in their subconscious minds, add everything that was modeled for them, and finally form their own opinions of the world. As they figure out who they are, we will often see the manifestations of what they encountered from birth to age fourteen. If we remind ourselves that the behaviors we see at this age are the result of what is in their subconscious minds and what was modeled for them, we can be more understanding when those behaviors are challenging.

Understanding the respective influence we have on our students at various grade levels is paramount as we help them overcome challenges, respond to obstacles, and develop their identities. Without that understanding, we may fail to recognize our role in their development.

When we incorporate coaching techniques in the classroom, we must remember that these developmental stages may have brought some negative paradigms into existence for many of our students. We must also remember that we may be unable to alter those beliefs in one school year, no matter how many minutes a day we spend with our students. We do make progress. We may not always see it, or it may take some time for us to recognize it, but again, it doesn't mean it isn't worth making the attempt. Progress is progress, after all.

I used to work with a person who seemed to have forgotten how difficult it was to be a kid. She would always express her surprise and dismay about the way our students acted.

I remember what it was like to be that age. I remember what an immature, goofy, hormonal mess I was as I became a teen and muddled through all the challenges that lay in front of me—and I had a really good home life with parents who were interested in and supportive of me. I cannot imagine what kind of lives some of our students live on a daily basis and the impact those environments must have on their ability to be the perfect teenagers as so many adults expect them to be.

RULE #1

Remember school and how tough it is to grow up—and cut the kids some slack.

As I stated earlier, being empathetic does not equal being a doormat. We can all sympathize with others without enabling them to use difficulties as a crutch.

I was really concerned when I started incorporating positivity into my life and classroom. I had established a classroom setting of no-nonsense where students knew they needed to do what they were told. I feared that being kind would make me weak and that students would try to take advantage of me and misbehave in my classroom.

After all, that is how I saw people who did not stand up for themselves. I used to think I had to have the last word and put people in their place, and if I didn't, they would walk all over me. I now know that controlling one's emotions is actually a sign of strength, not weakness.

First and foremost, the kinder I was to my students and the more genuine concern I showed them, the better they were for me. Being kind didn't make me a pushover. I still expect and strive to earn their respect.

The difference is that now they *want* to give their respect to me because I earned it. Before I gained it more out of the students' fear of what I might say or do. I like this new means of getting students to cooperate much better.

We must find a balance between kindness and authority. We can be sympathetic to a student's situation and still teach them how to persevere despite what they might be going through. The real world may or may not care if students are suffering personally, but the real world will definitely not allow that suffering to interfere with their job performance.

I have a friend who worked as an early childhood instructor. She worked for a friend of hers who owned her own business. My friend lost her ten-year-old daughter in a drowning incident. Six months after losing her child, her friend and boss let her go, stating that she was just "too sad" now. Again, the real world looks at the bottom line, and in many instances does not concern itself with what we are going through. It is unfair, but unfortunately, this is what often happens to people. Like the saying goes, "It's not personal, it's just business."

Taking our moods out on others and being unable to function professionally because something is bothering us personally is a great way to lose a job. Teaching students how to cope when they have a bad day is an imperative skill. Modeling that behavior for them ourselves is very important.

I bet you already knew that, right? Most of us have used the line, "How do you think your boss would respond if you spoke to him/her the way you just spoke to me now?" And how about, "What do you mean you don't have your assignment because you were absent when I handed it out? You are responsible for getting the work you miss. If you were absent the day you were supposed to get paid at work, would you just forget about the paycheck, or would you ask for it when you returned to work? Same idea!" Did those questions help the students change the behavior? Most likely not. That is where life coaching comes into play.

Asking questions is good. Asking condescending questions or being evidently disgruntled when we ask the questions, or using the questions to embarrass the student, is not so good. And, let's be honest, we weren't trying to win Teacher of the Year accolades when we posed those questions, were we?

Maybe instead you could ask, "If you were me, how would you handle what has happened here? Remember, everyone else was expected to turn in their work on time. My job is to prepare you for the real world, where you must do what your boss asks you to do and meet deadlines. So, what should I do in this situation?" This kind of question shows the student where you are coming from and puts the student in the position of authority, allowing, in most cases, for the victim mentality to be removed. Again, this is an example of a positive approach to the situation at hand. One size does not fit all, but this question can serve as an example of a better approach.

We must ask the right questions and ask them in the right way. The goal in asking the questions is to get the students to discover the right behavior themselves. If we talk down to them, if we tell them what they should be doing, they are not learning because it is not their idea.

Sometimes, especially when we ask the students questions in front of their peers, we know they will most likely respond in a smart-aleck way to save face. How we ask questions and where we ask them are oftentimes key to the success of those questions. It is up to us to figure out the right time and place to address a student.

It is important that we look at students individually to determine the best approach. However, as long as we are doing our best to make them safe, comfortable, and successful in our classrooms, we are doing our part to model the behaviors we expect from them, and we can use our positive behavior to curb their negative ones.

We may even be able to point out our positive behaviors to them and use those behaviors to get them to reflect on how they are treating us when we have been nothing but kind and fair with them. It allows them to see for themselves how their behavior toward us is undeserving.

We must break out of our own paradigms about dealing with students that were formed from our own experiences in the classroom and the way we were raised. We oftentimes resort to what is familiar even if it wasn't effective.

Take, for example, my high school friend. Her father used to physically abuse her mother. She hated it and hated him and cried about it all the time. Then, she dated a guy who physically abused her. She never broke away from what was familiar even though she hated it. She did not break out of that paradigm.

Coaching the student toward self-discovery takes a lot of time and work, and we already have so much on our plates, don't we? Our individual class sizes are huge, and the total number of students for whom we are instructionally responsible is often well over one hundred. Concepts and skills are continually added to our curriculum, but nothing is ever removed. It is much easier to simply scold the student for his/her poor behavior, maybe even fill out that referral for a detention and move on.

Furthermore, if we are tired, if we don't feel well, if we have our own personal issues to contend with, or if there is something at work that is bothering us, we are also apt to be less patient with our students and fall back into yelling and punishing them for their poor behaviors. It takes a lot of patience and energy to work on getting students to realize they need to make a change for the better.

So once again, before we can work on getting students to behave the way we want, we must first make sure we are okay. It's okay to have a bad day, but if every day is a bad day, we need to make a change within ourselves or change professions. If we are responsible for roughly 100 students every day for thirty-plus years, we are impacting three thousand or more lives. It is far too important of a job to allow our own agenda to have an adverse effect on the youth.

CHAPTER 2

How to Stay Positive in a Negative Setting

Simple Ways to Pump up Your Outlook and Your Environment

One of the most difficult tasks ever! Have you turned on the news? Have you ever ventured into the faculty room? You know that avoiding all negativity is absolutely impossible in our world. So, how can we stay positive in a negative setting?

First, we have to *decide* to be positive. When we make up our minds to do something, we can do it. Sometimes people believe that their mood or their day hinges on everyone else and their surroundings. Other people and bad circumstances definitely make it harder to stay in a positive state of mind, and again, it takes a great deal of work and self-control to do so. However, starting out our day the right way will have a huge impact on our success or failure with this endeavor.

I am not a morning person. Why I chose a profession that requires me to get up early every day is beyond me. The fact that I am high-maintenance and must get up early to start the process of getting ready is a whole other discussion in and of itself.

So, I rise at 4:30 a.m. every day. It used to be that the alarm went off and I cursed and hit the snooze button several times before I would eventually drag myself out of bed. I dreaded the fact that I was up and had to get ready to go to work.

I spent the day listening to and contributing to complaints about students, administration, rules, the building, and anything else I could find fault with at the time. My students were sometimes unruly, but most of the time they behaved out of fear—not because they respected or liked me as a human being. I didn't like my job as much then, and looking back, I didn't like myself a whole lot either. I wasn't the best me I could be, and I wasn't the best teacher. Oh, I did my job and had some successes, but was I performing at my best personally and professionally? I think not.

And what is the purpose of doing a job and not doing it well? A paycheck? Well, having enough money to live on and pay the bills is nice, but it isn't living. It is going through the motions and wasting precious time.

One truth that we all share is that none of us get out of this life alive. We get one shot to be us. Why not be the best "us" we can? We are not machinists making parts that can be scrapped and made again if we make a mistake. We are dealing with the lives of our youth, which have been entrusted to us. Our interactions can have profound effects on the people we educate.

Even the machinist, who can make a new part if a mistake is made, must make that part with the utmost precision and care. One-tenth of an inch off can make a part unusable. The machinist must be dead-on to ensure the part is of acceptable quality.

I believe people to be the same way. It is a must for us to be on and at our best before we can ever help our students. Working a forty-hour week, fifty weeks a year, from ages twenty-two to sixty-five adds up to about eighty-six thousand hours of your life. That is a lot of time to waste being mediocre.

And how are we living our best lives by robotically going through the motions? How are we going to discover our purpose? We are all here for a reason, and I do not believe that includes doing the bare minimum as we wait to die. How sad our existence would be if that was all this life was supposed to be.

One of the most important facts to remember is that we truly have more control over our days than we realize. Most people wake up and simply focus on dealing with everything as it happens to them. I used to feel like I was a knight in battle, putting up my shield all day long, trying to deflect whatever was coming at me. I did not start out my day with intention. I did not start out my day in a positive mindset.

I now take steps to make my day a positive one. First and foremost, I do not hit that snooze button, and one of the reasons is because I work very hard at getting a good night's rest. That concept is easier said than done—especially to those of us who have children. I used to sacrifice my own rest to get everything done because that was the only way there seemed enough hours in the day. But I did so at a cost because I was often short with people due to my exhaustion, and I would also wear my immune system down and waste even more time being sick in bed.

I don't have a surefire formula for you on how to get the rest you need because I am not walking in your shoes. (I would be a billionaire if I could come up with one solution to that dilemma that would work for everyone.) However, I can tell you what I know from experience, and that is:

RULE #2

You must take care of yourself, or you will not take care of anything else in your life properly.

Did you ever hear the statement that if the plane goes down, we must put the oxygen mask on ourselves first in order to be able to save anyone else? We can function without taking proper care of ourselves, but there is more to us than just functioning.

I have a clock that takes batteries. It keeps the time for me, but, as the batteries begin to lose their energy, the clock begins to lag behind a minute every day. Before I know it, in a month, it has lost about thirty minutes. When it is off by merely a minute or two, no one notices, but by the end of the month, when it is off by an entire thirty minutes, it becomes a problem. We can cheat ourselves and still make it all work, but eventually, it catches up with us.

We must figure out where we are losing time and try to find a solution to eliminate something that takes up too much of our day. If you are like me, you will insist there is nothing you can remove, but there is—we just have to look hard enough and *allow* ourselves the right to do so.

Our child does not need to be in dance, soccer, and Girl Scouts if it will run us ragged. We do not have to be the only one to take the neighbor's garbage out because he is old and cannot do it himself. We do not have to listen to our family and friends cry and complain because we need to be there for them. We do not have to like our friends' vacation pictures on social media so they do not get upset with us. We do not have to play golf with the guys twice a week so they keep asking us. We do not have to wash our car by hand each week to make the paint job last.

Do you see my point? Stop letting guilt or what you think you should do rule your life, and instead, do what you can do for you.

With that said, we must do our best to be rested so we are not tempted to hit that snooze button every morning. When we get up with our alarm, we should sit for a minute. We do not have to jump out of bed and start our day running. Stretch, breathe deeply, and then start your day off with a little gratitude.

Gratitude starts our day off the right way. We must recognize whether we view the glass as half-full or half-empty. If we are complaining about how we have to clean our windows this spring instead of being happy and grateful to have a house with windows to clean, part of the problem may be our own outlook. Are we happy and grateful to have a car to wash? A pet to walk? A job to go to?

It is how we rise each day, how we look at what we have, and how we give thanks for it that helps us ward off the negativity each of us faces on a daily basis. Starting our morning in a positive way helps keep us that way throughout the rest of our day.

I recently heard that Oprah starts off her day waking up and simply saying, "Thank you." I too have put this idea into practice.

Again, just because we start our day on a positive note does not mean we will not encounter negativity in our surroundings. It just means that we are better able to keep it in perspective and turn it around when we are faced with it.

And while starting off our day with an attitude of gratitude is definitely a good start, remember that gratitude throughout the day is a good idea too. It can be as simple as finding the perfect parking space at the grocery store and saying, "Thank you" aloud.

When my daughter was in second grade, I noticed that she was beginning to come to the dinner table complaining about her day. It was awful to look at this sweet little girl and hear such ugliness sounding from those tiny lips.

The sad part was the realization that she got it from my husband and me. We used to complain at the dinner table, and it is had rubbed off on our daughter. Hearing that negativity coming from a mere seven-year-old was a huge eye-opener. Immediately, we started going around the table and saying what we liked about our day and did not complain anymore. Some days it was difficult to muster up anything except that we were grateful that the sun was shining (and in Pennsylvania, that is a pretty rare occurrence), but it made all the difference for us and our daughter.

Soon, our daughter mirrored our more positive behavior. Notice that my husband and I modeled the behavior we wanted from her in place of telling her not to be so negative and reprimanding her for doing so.

Starting our day out the right way is imperative, but using this technique of being thankful for what we have all day long gives us another layer of protective armor to continue to ward off the negativity we encounter throughout the day. We cannot be in a bad mood and be in a grateful and happy mood at the same time. So, by keeping that practice going all day long, it will help us remain in a positive mindset despite what we may encounter.

Many of us are faced with a great deal of negativity on a daily basis. Teaching is not always viewed in a positive light in the public these days. Knowing that there is a negative public perception can be a barrier to feeling positive about our jobs and can make us feel defensive.

I hear teachers ranting about how difficult their jobs are to people who bash the profession. It is easy to want to defend our line of work to individuals who do not seem to have a clue about the challenges we face as educators.

I felt my shoulders sag with defeat when watching one of my favorite films, *Bad Moms*. The little girl in the movie was stressing about school and uttered something to the effect that her poor performance would result in her becoming a teacher. Ouch!

No matter how much we desire to fight back and defend the job we do, being defensive is not being positive. It would seem that we are arguing to change a negative point of view to a positive one, but arguing is never a positive and will most likely cause more hard feelings than do anything to change a person's mind. It can also lower our emotional intelligence. There are some people who thrive on upsetting others and baiting them into arguments. Those individuals are not looking to have a discussion with us and hear our perspective on the matter. They are only looking to incite us into arguing with them. Resist the temptation.

How do we combat the negativity against our profession? Part of that occurs when we are in a positive mindset as we head off to work and when we do our utmost to remain in that positive mindset all day long. Getting that good night's rest, waking up to the alarm without hitting snooze, stretching upon rising, making statements showing gratitude for the day and our job...all these acts will remind us that what we do matters—even if public perception is currently not as favorable toward us as we would like it to be.

And then, for some of us, there is the fear that is associated with our profession due to school shootings. For those of us working in the school system, personal harm is an all-too-real possibility. Next to workplace mass shootings, schools are the second most likely location in the nation for mass shootings to occur, according to Dr. Jim Warwick, who trained our school personnel on school shooting preparedness.

Looking at students and trying to discern which one might be the next to bring in a gun and harm us is an all-too-common thought process for teachers today. Is the detention I gave that kid going to push him over the edge and cause him to come after me? What would I do if our school were attacked?

First of all, fear is no way to live. We could be touring NYC or at a concert, the post office, or the mall, and some disgruntled individual could come in and shoot everyone there. It is a real epidemic everywhere. So are car accidents, but that doesn't mean we quit driving. Our chances of dying in a car accident are much greater than those of dying in a mass shooting. Still, the possibilities of harm or tragedy exist in education professions now more than ever. Concern and preparation are acceptable responses. Fear and overreaction are not.

Just knowing that a shooting is a threat in our profession can make the job more stressful. However, as difficult as it was to practice, having the active shooter training at our school, not once or twice, but three times now, has helped tremendously. Being prepared makes that threat a little easier to handle. Further, it also allows for muscle memory, which makes us less likely to panic and more likely to respond accordingly.

If your school or workplace has not had this type of training, you may wish to suggest it to your employer. If you are able to enlist someone for this purpose, please do your homework and get someone in with the right credentials so that you will be properly trained. Knowledge is power, and being knowledgeable about school/work safety will be one way to deter this stressor.

Exposure to negative people creates another stressor. Whenever we can, we should avoid being around negative people at work. Of course, this isn't always possible, especially in such environments as faculty meetings, training sessions, and so forth, but you can put space between yourself and negative people at other times of the day, such as during lunch, in the copy room, or after work. If we work with people who dislike their job and complain about it and other aspects of their lives, we should steer clear of those individuals whenever possible.

We become like the five people we are around the most, so putting ourselves in professional or social situations with people who are negative will do nothing to help us stay in a positive state of being. It can be lonely if most of our staff are not positive, but it is always possible to find people who are not always complaining and know how to be grateful. It may make us change where we eat lunch and who we sit with during in-services, and that is not always a comfortable change to make, but I am betting that the more positive we become, the more we will begin to dislike being around those people anyway.

Next, practice positive self-talk. Our subconscious mind does not know the word "not." If we are going around saying, "I will not get upset with my students today," "I will not hit my snooze button," "I will not resort to chocolate and coffee to survive fifth period," we will get more out of it because we are focusing on what we do not want. And, whatever receives our focus will keep happening. We have a tendency to discuss what we don't want in our lives instead of focusing on and discussing what we do want. Instead of telling ourselves we won't get upset with our students, we could say, "I will be in a good mood today." The way we speak has a profound effect on our ability to be positive. When we want something positive to happen, say something positive. Make it a point to turn around negative self-talk.

One way to improve negative self-talk is to say something nice each morning as we look in the mirror. How many of us drag ourselves into the bathroom, take a look in the mirror, and think, *Whoa, look at how awful I look this morning.* We look at the dark circles, wrinkles, and puffiness of our bloodshot eyes, our gray hairs, age spots, saggy skin, untoned physique, our mussed-up hair, etc. We focus on all the physical features we view about ourselves in a negative light. Why not change our focus and concentrate on what is wonderful about us? Albeit, it is incredibly difficult to look in the mirror at 4:30 a.m. and say, "Wow, you are stunning." Feels like a lie, and maybe at that very moment, it is in fact an untrue utterance. However, saying something nice instead of criticizing ourselves is a much better way to start our day—however untrue it may seem. Again, it puts us in a more positive mindset to start our day.

Along the same lines as getting adequate rest, treat your body well. I am not saying give up caffeine and chocolate and only eat fruits and vegetables and chicken and fish and drink water and exercise like a fiend—we just need to take better care of ourselves. Those steps can be as simple or as challenging as we would like them to be based on the results we want to see.

One simple step we can take to improve overall wellness is to breathe. We do not breathe properly—especially when we are stressed. Life coaches teach people to breathe deeply by filling their lungs to capacity, taking a deep breath in through their nose, holding it for a few seconds, and then slowly releasing it through their mouths. Do that exercise, at the very least, three times.

Visualization alongside these breathing exercises will further improve the effects of this type of breathing. If you are in a place where you can close your eyes, do so. First, think of your happiest memory, then close your eyes and picture that memory as you practice this breathing exercise.

If you are in a place where you can also try the technique I describe below in conjunction with the breathing technique and visualization I described above, it will help relieve your anxiety and stress even more.

If you are right-handed, take your left hand and put your left hand flat against your body, between your breast and throat, with your fingers pointing toward the left side of your body. Then put your right hand flat against your body, on the lower part of your stomach, with your fingers outstretched toward the right side of your body. Close your eyes, think of your happiest memory, and take those three, deep breaths.

This technique helps to ground you as you do these visualization and breathing exercises. Many people who suffer from anxiety and panic attacks use this method of breathing to prevent the attacks or to recover after an attack.

And, if we are so inclined to eat better and get some form of exercise and stay hydrated by drinking water, then those habits will serve to help us as well. I know drinking beverages when teaching is often neglected because of our limited bathroom visits, but using your better judgment, we should drink water as much as we can.

The same goes for exercise. Using common sense about movement is key. When some people think of exercise, they think they have to join a gym and get on the Stairmaster for an hour, and only after dripping with sweat feel like they have accomplished something. For some people, this vision is what they think of when someone says exercise is important. If you like that type of physical fitness, more power to you.

However, if you are like many other people who find that type of exercise grueling and who feel they do not have the time to devote to it, you should simply walk more and move more. My husband read an article that said sitting is the new smoking. Movement is good. Period. You decide what that looks like for you, but the key here is to simply move more.

If you are using tobacco products or drinking a lot of alcohol, I don't have to tell you that those habits are not serving you to be the best person you can be. However, it is up to you how much you want your life to change and what you are willing to do to make those changes. Sincerely reflect on it and decide if those habits are impeding your ability to excel in any way and then determine what you want to do about it if anything.

The most important thing to remember is that if we try to do everything all at one time, the chances of sticking to a new routine will be very slim. Change is difficult and can be overwhelming. If positive changes are stressing us out, maybe we are doing too much at one time or putting too much pressure on ourselves.

I made up my mind that I was going to exercise more, but I got to the point where I was upset if I had anything to do after work because I would have to exercise too late and I was tired by then. I gave myself permission to miss on those nights. I decided that if it was causing me stress to do something good, I should cut myself some slack. I do not make excuses. That is totally different than giving myself a pass when it causes me angst.

You know yourself best. You know what you should do to keep yourself healthy and happy and whole. Just be honest with yourself and make a plan that you can keep. The key is having a plan and working to stick with it. Give yourself a little leeway if your plan is too rigid as well.

Now, most of us just say we are going to do something, but we don't stick with it. I have said to myself for a couple of years now that I am going to run a half-marathon at the end of summer, and I haven't done it yet. This year, I have told people I am doing it next September, have asked a friend to join me, and have put it down in writing. I downloaded a marathon training app and discovered a half-marathon that takes place locally at the end of every summer. My next step is to fill out the application and pay the sign-up fee. I believe that by taking these steps, I will actually follow through with my goal and run the half-marathon next summer. For me, that is how I make a plan and stick to it. Know what motivates you and keeps you on track so that you can implement a plan and follow it.

That is why we have students write out their goals and revisit them. One way to create a plan and stick with it is to make a vision board.

I use vision boards to accomplish my own goals and to help students accomplish theirs. For some, a vision board is a large board with pictures of goals on it.

I decided that the best vision board for me and my students would be something more portable. Many of my students do not stay in the same place every night, so placing their goals on an actual poster board would not easily allow them to bring the board to class or take it with them wherever they are staying that night. I have my students write their goals on a piece of paper. Then, I have them find pictures to correspond with their written goals. They may draw pictures, cut pictures from a magazine or newspaper, print them from the internet, and/or use three-dimensional objects, and so forth. They then adhere these pictures/objects to an 8.5 x11 piece of cardstock.

I put mine in a notebook, which allows me to transport my vision board without damaging it and lets me add a new vision board each year. Having the old one in there enables me to see what I have achieved and helps remind me that I still have goals to conquer. It also lets me see how much I have changed over the years.

Reviewing my vision boards can also reveal that I may need to alter goals that no longer fit who I am and who I want to be. My earlier goal of learning to play the fiddle to "Devil Went Down to Georgia" is no longer a goal of mine (don't judge). I have a few silly goals in my vision board book (as you now know) and some serious ones. I was able to check off riding a mechanical bull, but I have not checked off being a published author for Blue Mountain Arts Card Company (yet!). So, I'll add the Blue Mountain Arts author goal again next year and will do so until I achieve it or it is no longer my goal. I have my students spend about three minutes each day looking at their vision boards.

I play music from YouTube that stimulates the mind as they concentrate on their boards. The music helps relax them and acts as a timer for the three minutes they must concentrate on their boards. When the music begins, they become quiet, and when the music ends, they know they are done. I encourage them to see the goals as if they have already accomplished them.

Visualization is a huge component to making goals a reality. It helps you believe that you can and will do what you set out to do. I encourage students to use their five senses as they visualize their goal.

When I picture an event from my vision board, I see it happening to me. I go so far as to concentrate on what I am wearing, what sounds I hear around me, what smells are associated with achieving that goal, what I can feel at that moment, and sometimes, even what I can taste. The more we use our five senses in the visualization process, the more real and attainable the goal becomes.

Beyond that, seeing myself living the life I want to live *as if it has already happened* as I use my vision board is also an effective way to ensure that I am truly immersed in the goals I have set before me in picture form. I allow myself to feel the joy, the pride that will be mine from accomplishing these goals. This type of focus helps bring my goals to fruition.

While students are spending those three minutes looking at their vision boards, I will sometimes take attendance. Mostly, I look at my own vision board when they are looking at their boards so that I am modeling the behavior I expect from them. It is a good time to take three quiet minutes for myself to regroup and get in a positive mindset for that group of students.

Once we finish our time with our vision boards, sometimes we play what I call, "Let's Pretend." We set aside five minutes or less to talk about our goals as if they had already happened. We start with, "I am so happy and grateful that I…" and then finish the sentence with a statement about what we have accomplished. Some students have talked about passing their driver's tests, getting a job they want, getting an "A" on a test, and so on. Some days I had to put on a timer to end it because so many participated, and other days, crickets. I often shared my own "Let's Pretend" with them too. The funny part was that I was so convincing that a lot of them would stop me and ask if "that" really happened. This exercise was an extension of our visualization. Using our imaginations in this way drives home the impact of putting feeling behind what we see on our vision boards.

And just how does what we see impact our well-being? I love the line from the movie *The Blind Side* when Leigh Anne asks Michael how he got out of his negative environment without letting it consume him the way it had for so many other boys from the same part of town with similar living conditions.

Michael responds by saying, "When I was little, and something awful was happening, Mama would tell me to close my eyes. She was trying to keep me from seeing her do drugs or other bad things. When she was finished, and the bad things were over, she would say, 'Now, I'm going to count to three, and you open your eyes. The past is gone. The world is a good place and it's all going to be okay.'" He didn't succumb to his environment because his mother made him close his eyes. He didn't see the bad images before him. As much as she failed him in so many other ways, she gave him a gift when she forced him not to witness the negativity surrounding him.

We all know that there is bad in the world, and I am not suggesting we make ourselves ignorant to it by putting blinders over our eyes. But how much we expose ourselves to it and when we watch it is incredibly important to our well-being.

What are you watching or doing right before you go to bed? Did you know that the last forty-five minutes before you go to sleep are the most important to getting proper rest and keeping your mind positive? Not that I don't love shows like *Monsters Inside Me* or *Law & Order: SVU*, but watching that right before crashing for the night may not be the best-laid plan.

Watching anything negative is a bad idea, particularly before we rest. And watching the news keeps us informed, but how informed do we need to be? I know people who have CNN running day and night in their homes. They watch the same negative stories told in a myriad of ways over and over again. Does that keep us informed or in a negative mindset?

How about technology? There are studies that suggest too much technology before we attempt to rest can also impede our ability to shut down our minds and sleep soundly. I'm not suggesting that we sit and stare at a wall before we turn in for the night, but finding a way to unwind that involves something upbeat will definitely help us rest better and keep our mind positive.

I will read a good book, drink a cup of tea, take a hot bath, do some stretching or self-reflecting, or cuddle with my husband or dog before I turn in for the night. If you have to break the rule and watch something, be sure it is something positive. For example, if you really want to watch television, make sure that uplifting or funny programming is on your itinerary.

Which brings me to my next suggestion—smile! When I first read how important it is to smile, I realized how unnatural it was for me. I felt like everyone would be looking at me wondering what I was up to if I smiled all the time.

Now, I don't suggest being fake. The first thing many people say when I suggest that they smile more is that they are doing it because I told them they should, not because they want to or have something to smile about. Initially, it may feel fake or strained, but as with all of these practices, the more you do it, the better you will feel, and the more natural it will become.

I have made myself smile on days when all I wanted to do is cry, and I was astonished at how differently I began to see what was making me want to cry. It is impossible to be truly miserable with a smile on your face.

Did you ever hear the line, "Fake it till you make it?" I read somewhere that if you are unhappy, you should pretend to be happy. You should do anything you believe that a happy person would do, and in doing so, you will actually begin to feel happier. If that means you have to put a smile on your face when you want to frown, that is what you should do. When I put this concept into practice myself, the sadness I was facing became less important to me as I enjoyed my smile more than that feeling of wanting to cry. In the end, the happiness won over my sadness. It made choosing to be happy an easier task.

I know you have heard the phrase, "Actions speak louder than words." So, watch your facial expressions. Do not cross your arms over your chest as you stand in the hallway waiting for the students to file into your classroom. When you smile and keep your arms uncrossed and greet the students warmly as they walk into your room, you are showing them that you like yourself, your job, and them. If we wish for our students to believe that we care about them, and if we want them to feel welcome in our classrooms, we should show these things with our nonverbal and verbal cues.

If we are frowning and come across as unhappy to be at work, how can we expect our students to want to come to our classrooms, pay attention to us, and learn from us? We have all had experiences with the grumpy, miserable teacher and/or professor who so obviously should have made another career choice. Did you get excited to go to that person's class or dread it?

It is time to evaluate how your own demeanor and expressions are impacting the learning environment of your students. Oh, I know it is difficult to be sunshine and butterflies when you have a group of unruly, disinterested students coming to your classroom. I also know that when you are having personal problems or don't feel well, it makes it all the harder to come to work and be okay. We are human beings, not robots. But, if you like your job, and your desire is to reach your students, you must find a way to be joyful while you are there.

As union vice president for eight years and union president for the past three of them, I have had so many people come to me complaining about everything and anything they perceive to be wrong with our school. Do not get me wrong; there is always room for improvement, and many of the issues that have been brought to me have merit. However, when we focus on what we don't like about what is happening on the job, it does not improve our situation but oftentimes makes it more difficult to come to work and enjoy what we do.

No matter what is happening in our lives, what we focus on will bring more of that to us. Did you ever hear the saying, "When it rains, it pours?" That is because when we pour all our energy into what is bothering us, we draw more negative experiences to us. That is why it is vital to our well-being, and therefore the well-being of our students and the people around us, that we work hard to keep our focus on our blessings and not our burdens.

One way to put our focus back in the right place is through the practice of meditation. Meditation is a practice that has gained new momentum over the past several years. It has been in existence for centuries but has only more recently started to gain acceptance as mainstream in the United States.

I learned the importance of meditation in my life coaching class. Starting my day off in silent contemplation for twenty minutes did make a difference in helping me remain calm. The problem I had with it was that I could never seem to keep my mind from wandering. I tried silent meditation, guided meditation, clearing my mind, focusing on my breathing—you name it, I tried it. I just could not get my mind cleared every time, and when I was unable to do so, I felt like a failure.

Further, I was not always in a place where I could be alone or where it was quiet to do the meditation. So, I drifted away from it. I knew it was good for me, but I felt like something was missing.

I record *The Ellen DeGeneres Show* since it comes on during the day when I am at work. I turned it on one Sunday when I was cooking, and what she said stopped me in my tracks. Ellen introduced Bob Roth, the author of *Strength in Stillness: The Power of Transcendental Meditation*. She went on to discuss transcendental meditation with Mr. Roth and admitted that she practices TM and has been doing so since 2010. I listened to the rest of the show and ordered the book that same day.

I devoured the book and became convinced that I wanted to learn TM and maybe even become a TM teacher. I looked for TM teachers near me, found one in a city only two hours away, and signed up for the course. I took the class and was hooked.

What I loved about TM is that the practice of it is effortlessness. You can do it on a train, a bus, on a bench at the mall, or in the privacy of your home. And, it's okay if your mind wanders. It does not mean you are not doing it "right." There is no right or wrong way to do it. You just do it as it comes to you. For me, this meditation was exactly what I had been seeking.

TM has worked well for me. And it works for countless others. In Bob Roth's book, mentioned above, he discusses a CEO named Bill. After Bill began practicing TM, one of Bill's colleagues said, "You're so much calmer, more patient, more present, less reactive, and your perspective seems so much more balanced and assertive in a thoughtful way. Your meditation is good for everyone." Think about that statement. It was "good for everyone." My own family knows when I haven't meditated and actually encourages me to do it.

Ellen isn't the only famous person who meditates with TM. George Harrison practiced TM for years. Clint Eastwood and Jerry Seinfeld practice TM. Celebrities in the limelight such as Ellen and these individuals know the importance of taking that quiet time of calm for themselves.

TM is also helping people who suffer from Post-Traumatic Stress Disorder. According to Google, 44.7 million people have this disorder. Eight percent of Americans suffer from PTSD, and 24.4 percent of people have had it at any given time. This number equals the size of Texas.

Military personnel suffer most frequently from this disorder. However, other people who have experienced trauma can also develop it. Not everyone who experiences a trauma gets PTSD. Everyone processes experiences differently, and for that reason, the support someone receives after a traumatic experience often determines if they end up with PTSD. The disorder is very commonplace for people who have experienced physical or sexual assault.

The good news is that TM helps people afflicted with PTSD, particularly military personnel. I have read that many active-duty military personnel suffering from PTSD have been able to use TM to reduce or eliminate the use of many of the psychotropic drugs prescribed to them to combat its debilitating symptoms.

Think then about the number of our students and/or their family members who may be suffering from PTSD. It is imperative to practice meditation for our own well-being and so we can be at our best to help our students. As I have stated, TM is the meditative practice that works best for me, but simply finding a meditative practice and sticking with it is what is important for you. As Bob Roth in his book on TM said, "Meditating does not mean that life's unexpected challenges and obstacles suddenly disappear. It does mean, however, that you will be better equipped to take on those challenges with greater energy, focus, and resilience."

Wouldn't it be great if schools began adopting meditation as a common practice for students and staff? I have seen studies about schools incorporating yoga as a means of helping kids find calm. Until school-wide efforts are made to help students obtain a calmer state, practicing meditation yourself, and if you feel comfortable doing so, sharing that experience with your students, can help inspire them to attempt meditation too. Feeling good is an important part of doing well. Meditation is just one step toward feeling your best.

You have no doubt heard people say they have become addicted to the feeling that vigorous exercise gives them. That is the adrenaline rush it gives you. I believe that those feelings also occur when you live in a more positive mindset. It feels better to be happy. After we have been working to be happier and start to feel bad again, we like going back to our positive state of mind. We start to realize it's actually better there.

Unfortunately, our subconscious mind can make it difficult for us to do because even though we feel better when we are happy, returning to what is familiar is often very tempting. People often set themselves up for failure only so they can say things like, "See? I'm not meant to be happy."

I had a friend in high school whose father used to say that his daughter "wasn't happy unless she was unhappy." In the same way people get addicted to those positive feelings, some people get addicted to the attention they get when they have a problem.

I know people who post on social media every negative thing that happens to them. I swear, they do it just so they can get sympathy for it. I love the people who write the cryptic messages hoping everyone will beg them to say what is wrong like, "Why does this always happen to me?!" Then you see a whole line of posts saying, "What's wrong?" "What happened?" "Aw, praying for you." It's important to see that behavior for what it is and steer clear of it—for yourself and from those so-called friends. Those kinds of people are not the five individuals we should associate with as we strive to become the best person we can be.

So, smile as much as possible. When you find it incredibly difficult to do so, find something positive that makes you smile. While eating a huge hunk of chocolate cake may make you feel good in the moment, it will not have a lasting effect. The temptation here is to indulge in a quick fix. You need to remember to do what makes you feel good for more than the moment you do it. If it turns into a negative feeling after the fact, you did not find something truly positive to make you happy.

I always recommend watching a YouTube or TikTok video with babies laughing or pets doing something silly. Most of us have smartphones and other technology at our fingertips, making it easier than ever to pull up a funny video and watch it when we need it.

I started this practice a few years ago and have incorporated it in my classroom. I do not do it every day but will often start class with a funny or cute video. It gets me in the right mindset to teach and helps students find the right frame of mind to be positive and learn.

On *The TODAY Show*, I saw that they are showing cute video clips that they refer to as a morning boost. Lester Holt of *NBC Nightly News* is showcasing people who did more than was expected of them in a Friday report called, "Above and Beyond." Positivity in news reporting is beginning to gain momentum as people recognize the need for positive news. If you like to start your day with the news, watching a positive clip from one of these news affiliates or on YouTube is a good way to do it.

Positive or funny images can put us in a better frame of mind as well. I use a picture of my husband taking his first selfie in front of the Eiffel Tower in Paris as my phone's wallpaper. He had no clue what he was doing and looks absolutely stunned in the picture, but I love it. Not because I am making fun of him for taking this shot where he looks so silly, but because I think it is so incredibly cute that he had no clue what he was doing. When I look at that picture, it makes me smile and recall a wonderful trip of a lifetime with the people I love.

Surround yourself in your classroom or office with what makes you smile if you have the means to buy it and are allowed to put it up at work. I realize that this suggestion seems extravagant when many schools cannot afford pencils and teachers are providing these supplies using their own paltry wages, but if it is a possibility, it can help you and your students.

I also realize I am blessed to have a classroom. Some of you are traveling teachers with no space of your own, going from room to room. Creating a workspace like I describe here may not be an option for some. However, maybe decorating the cart you take with you from room to room or putting something in each classroom you visit might be an option. The key here is to surround yourself with *anything that you can* that will make you happy in your workspace. I worked in my laundry room when we were working from home in March 2020, and for the remainder of the school year, I tried to make the space as user-friendly as possible, adding a lamp and a plug-in air freshener with my favorite vanilla and cinnamon scent. I also put a corkboard on the wall in front of my computer so that I could put pictures and sayings on it that would keep me feeling upbeat.

I keep photos of my family around at work. I have a salt lamp on my filing cabinet to give off positive ions. And just as I did in my home workspace during our virtual instructional time, I now have a corkboard with all kinds of sayings, drawings, photos, and such hanging right in front of my computer at work. I change what I put on it from year to year, basing my choices on what I like to see while I am working. I also keep both real and fake plants around my room for some life and color. I have a small fountain that sits in the corner of my room. I also have a number of pieces of artwork hung around my classroom.

My administrators are so awesome—they allowed me to have students from our art class paint positive quotes on the walls in my classroom. I currently have ten quotes on my walls, from a Ben Franklin favorite, "Tell me and I forget, teach me and I may remember, involve me and I learn," to one from Harry Potter Headmaster, Albus Percival Wulfric Brian Dumbledore, that says, "Words are, in my not-so-humble opinion, our most inexhaustible source of magic, capable of both inflicting injury and amending it."

While your surroundings are important, taking the time to "take in" your surroundings is equally so. Sometimes we take our surroundings for granted and need to take inventory of the beauty around us.

My family has to drive over the breast of a lake dam to get home. One evening, I was running through my head all the things I needed to do as I was driving my daughter home from the sitter's house when she was just six years old. When we began to cross the dam, my daughter said, "Mommy, look at how pretty the sky and the water looks." I actually pulled off to the side of the road to take a look at it. She was right. It looked stunning.

And you know what? If it weren't for my daughter, I would have missed it. Take inventory of the beauty around you and find beauty in the ashes. If your classroom or office looks too sterile or unfriendly, see what you can do about it.

Feng shui is a study that involves the arrangement of living space to create harmony and peace in our lives. The classroom environment is imperative to the well-being of both us and our students. According to Jack Canfield and Harold C. Wells in their book *100 Ways to Enhance Self-Concept in the Classroom*, they say that "…the physical environment in a classroom can influence the way a child feels about himself and others, as well as his attitude toward school in general."

Feng shui is not a simplistic practice. It is truly multi-faceted. There are entire books dedicated to the practice and varying types of feng shui, from Chinese to Western. To teach you how to incorporate it in your life inside this text would be overreaching on my part. However, I can give you some of the basic concepts, and if it seems to interest you, you could take it a step further and find some materials that would go into more depth with you.

I took a short evening course on it and studied the materials I was given and incorporated the practice into the arrangement of my home and classroom. I noticed that much of what I studied, I was already doing in my classroom. I had been incorporating feng shui without knowing it. In Western feng shui, there is a *helpful people* section. In my classroom, that section of the room is where I had placed my desk. In the *creativity and children* section of the room, I had placed student artwork. For the *wealth and prosperity* section, the course recommended a water fountain for that section of the room, and I had one there already. I was pleased that I seemed to have a natural affinity for creating a balanced space.

According to Jayme Barnett, the author of *Feng Shui Your Life*, "everything in your outer surroundings affects the course of your life." He also says that your surroundings reflect your "health, work, and relationships, as well as to your everyday interactions." Feng shui is simply another avenue that helps us achieve balance and harmony within and in our surroundings.

Feng shui also promotes the idea that we need to be in sync inwardly for success to be achieved outwardly. Making changes to our environment won't work until we make changes to us. It is the same as trying to change our students instead of changing ourselves—they will not change until we do. Inner feng shui requires that we hone our intuition, gratitude, and positivity, among other things.

Often, our external environments are a reflection of what is happening internally. Have you ever watched the show *Hoarders*? I feel sorry for these individuals, but I am fascinated by how they live their lives and the reasons behind it. The hoard always has to do with what is going on with them emotionally. They experience a loss of some kind and cling to "things" since they cannot keep what they lost, which is typically a person who left them due to death or sometimes through abandonment or divorce. They cling to the hoard, driving those who may still be part of their lives further away from them. Their external chaos is a reflection of their internal chaos.

Look around you. Is there clutter? Do you hold onto items "just in case" you might need them again? Is your home, car, and/or classroom jam-packed with obsolete items? Is it disorderly? Maybe if you declutter your life physically you can make some changes emotionally. As Barnett states, "Our external environments, like our homes, can sometimes reflect our internal states. There can be an emotional connection between the seen (our homes) and the unseen (our inner state)."

As such, it is important to look around at your physical environment to see if it provides you with feedback about what is happening in your internal environment. If we want our students to learn and grow when in our charge, we must provide an environment that allows our students to do so. Making sure that our classroom reflects our goals for our students by keeping it organized, bright, and cheerful will help us achieve our personal and professional goals.

Bill Strickland is the author of the book *Make the Impossible Possible*. Bill was a student at a school in the north side of Pittsburgh, Pennsylvania, where he attributes art to saving his life. After earning fifteen honorary doctorates from universities such as Carnegie Mellon University and Westminster College, Bill has opened schools in some of the worst areas of our country. These schools, which are nationally accredited and state-licensed adult-training centers, offer adult students a free education to help them earn higher-paying jobs to feel better about themselves.

Bill makes sure that the learning environment these people attend is aesthetically pleasing. His company is known as the Manchester Bidwell Corporation, and their philosophy is simple: *environment shapes behavior.* Their schools are constructed with the idea of creating "an empowering atmosphere of art, light, music, and a staff that strives to realize the genius in everyone." The idea is simple—create an environment where people feel good, and they will want to learn. Bill Strickland recognizes that where you learn is just as important as what you learn.

Keep close tabs on how you are tending to the learning environment you inhabit. Not only will it impact your students, but chances are you spend more time in your classroom than you do in your home, so making sure it is an inviting place for you to go and for your students to learn is an imperative part of your journey to keeping a positive outlook.

Color is also vital to creating the environment you wish to create. You may not be able to change the color of the walls of your classroom, but the use of color to add to the feeling created by it in your teaching space is an important aspect of creating a positive work environment for you and a positive learning environment for your students.

According to a number of experts, colors make people feel a certain way. Blue is a calming color; it represents trustworthiness and security. Yellow, in small doses, is energizing, warm, and stimulating, while its use in larger doses makes people uneasy. Think about the feeling you wish to create in your classroom and utilize as much of that color as you can to create the optimal space for your coaching classroom.

Did you notice that when our president wishes to convey his power to us he wears a red tie? When he wants us to be calm and feel secure he wears a blue tie? This is not an accident. These color choices are made with the knowledge of the feelings the colors evoke in us. It is not just a Republican-red and Democrat-blue color choice.

Similarly, restaurant ads use a lot of orange. Orange is supposed to create feelings of hunger in people. Green represents nature and money, so recycling symbols are green, as is the logo for H&R Block. Again, these color choices are not accidental and should show you how important the use of color is to your living- and workspace. If politicians and multi-million dollar companies, both of which wish to influence us, understand and use colors to their advantage, educators should recognize the importance of the use of color in our workspace and use it to create the learning environment we desire.

All of these steps are helpful in getting us ready to help our students reach their full potential. When we are striving to be our best, we can then expect the best from our students and provide them with a learning environment that leads them to discover all they are capable of becoming while making our time in that environment better for ourselves as well.

CHAPTER 3

But What About the Curriculum?

*Strategies to Help You Balance Academia
and Coaching in the Classroom*

We are all inundated by the pressure to finish teaching the textbook and ensure students are ready for their standardized tests. How can you spend time coaching students in the classroom without compromising the time allotted for the curriculum?

In my school, we currently teach in a block schedule where we see our classes every other day for eighty-minute periods. I can tell you that even when we have a lot of material to cover, I will spend time coaching students each class period. I have found that if I spend just a few minutes or sometimes as much as fifteen of an eighty-minute period coaching them before we begin the lesson or assignment, they tend to work harder in the fifty-five minutes I have left as opposed to not coaching them and setting aside the full eighty-minute period to teach the curriculum.

RULE #3

You will get more quality work from students when the lessons are both life and academic lessons.

Make no mistake that this concept of *The Coaching Classroom* is a balancing act. We should not neglect well-being for the sake of the curriculum, and focusing on the student's well-being should never cause us to neglect the curriculum. I know a teacher who focuses on many of the concepts of *The Coaching Classroom* in her course but has seriously neglected teaching the curriculum.

The goal of *The Coaching Classroom* is to get students in the right frame of mind to learn so that it is easier to then teach them the core content. It is showing students you care in place of going through the motions of the lesson without making any meaningful connections with them.

I have found that students who know we care and want what is best for them, as a rule, are more readily willing to work for us than students who see us as simply a facilitator doling out the required lessons.

Do not try to fool them into thinking you care. The key here is that you must be sincere. If you attempt to apply my methods and deep down hate the students and/or hate the job, they will sense it and swarm in like piranha stripping your flesh to the bone and exposing you for the fraud that you are.

Now, I am not saying that we have to love every aspect of our career and every student to make *The Coaching Classroom* work. Just like the positive self-talk where we look in the mirror every day and tell ourselves that we are handsome or beautiful—sometimes it starts out as a lie.

Sometimes I wake up in the morning and tell myself that today is going to be the best day of my life, and I feel like I am fibbing to myself because I know we have a faculty meeting that morning and that we will be discussing unpleasant topics. I know that I have my most difficult student today and that I have a parent-teacher conference with a disgruntled parent after classes are dismissed. I know what lies ahead of me, and yet I am telling myself it is going to be the best day of my life.

Feels like a lie at that point. But, I don't say it as a means of making all of those encounters go away. I say it so that my mind is in the right place to deal with what I am about to face with the faculty meeting, the student, the parent, and any other unexpected trial that comes my way.

You may have no problem showing five out of six classes how much you appreciate them. But then there is that one class, with that handful of students who, when scheduled together, can be an enormous challenge at best. You wonder how to maintain your composure, manage the class effectively, and complete the lessons. And now you are expected to incorporate life coaching techniques as well?

One bit of advice a dear, wise friend gave me that has helped me with that kind of a class is to "love the unlovable." Simple concept, but incredibly difficult to put into practice.

Here is the fact of the matter. It is easy to be a great teacher to great students. They would be good even if they had a lousy teacher standing in front of them. The kids who need us are, most likely, the ones who push our buttons the most. So, we need to "love the unlovable." It is one of the most difficult aspects of my job that I have attempted to tackle and yet also the most rewarding. I sometimes think that challenging individuals are put in our path to teach us something about ourselves. If we can look at those encounters we have with our challenging students as a lesson to us in patience, kindness, tolerance, etc., it won't seem like a burden but quite possibly a blessing in disguise.

I had a student who performed poorly academically in my class and who got in trouble at school. I really thought she was a lost cause, but then I was absolutely surprised. Our administration organizes an activity every year in which they give the students cards and ask them to write a note to a teacher or teachers who made a difference in their lives. Then, they put the notes in our mailboxes for Teacher Appreciation Day.

Well, guess who wrote a card for me telling me I was helping her turn her life around? Yep, the kid I thought I wasn't reaching. I was fortunate enough to get that immediate feedback with that student. As I mentioned earlier, the downside to trying *The Coaching Classroom* can be the lack of immediate positive feedback or never getting any feedback at all. However, I have found that since incorporating life coaching techniques in my classroom setting, I receive more immediate positive feedback now than ever before.

When I first started teaching, I was such a fool. I used to think that everyone was raised like me. I believed that if a student acted up in school it was because the student was bored and just trying to give the teacher a hard time for the fun of it.

Eventually, I learned that while there were a few kids who did in fact misbehave for fun, I didn't need to blame myself and assume that most kids misbehaved as a result of my subpar lesson. I found that most of their disruptive behaviors were a result of something much different than an attempt to upset the apple cart.

Anyone in education knows why kids often misbehave in class—trying to hide a learning deficit, living in a dysfunctional environment, using drugs or alcohol, starving for attention, just to name a few. And again, I am not in any way saying it is excusable for someone to act poorly because of their situation.

I read the novel *A Child Called "It"* and three of Dave Pelzer's other memoirs. In his book *Help Yourself,* the fifth book in the series, I love how he discusses how he has made it in this life even after growing up and being labeled as the victim of one of the worst child abuse cases in the United States. He could easily use his upbringing as a reason behind every failure in his life. Instead, he says, "I don't blame others for my problems. I stand on my own. I won't waste my life away."

Students may have legitimate reasons for being stressed and upset. Many are living in peril. I think worse than that are the students who are growing up in unhealthy environments and do not know it because it is all they've been exposed to. Showing them images and reading to them about people who grew up in environments that placed obstacles in front of them and then showing the students how these people not only survived their upbringing but thrived in spite of it is essential.

Many people have this terrible habit of using any obstacle as a crutch as to why they are not living up to their full potential. It is our job to teach our students to use adversity to their advantage, to not blame anyone except themselves for their shortcomings. The truth of the matter is that we all face difficulties in life. Someone will always have it better, and someone will always have it worse. We have a choice. We can let it control us or let it inspire us to do better.

We have far too many students who have "learned helplessness," where they never take responsibility for their actions. It has actually become a societal norm. Reminding them to take responsibility for their actions using literature, such as Dave Pelzer's book, is one way to get them to see the importance of facing their problems and fixing them.

If students do not deal with the issues that are having an adverse effect on them, they will most likely fail to excel academically no matter how fantastic our lesson may be. Supplementing our curriculum with coaching classroom techniques takes a step in addressing the concept of getting students to face what ails them. It is not taking away time from the curriculum but enhancing it.

And remember, the way we treat them can have a profound impact on how willing they are to behave in our classroom and learn from us. We all get frustrated and react instead of responding to our students. However, I see far too many educators imposing punishments and speaking to their students in a manner that is destructive and ineffective. The curriculum won't matter if they don't feel they matter to us.

Such a response to student behavior occurs mostly because educators themselves are frustrated and don't know what else to do. And, in managing our classrooms in such a manner, we might get some of our worst students out of our hair for a while. After all, that is what a referral does for us—the student gets removed from our charge for a few days when the offense is serious enough. But what are we going to get when the student returns?

Did the student have some kind of epiphany while he/she was out of our rooms during in-school suspension or out-of-school suspension? Or, as the kid is sitting in detention, does the kid say to him/herself, "Hey, if I don't want to sit in detention, be assigned in-school suspension, or sit at home in an out-of-school suspension, I'd better be good the next time I am in that class." Hardly the conversation the student has with him/herself.

There have only been a handful of success stories that have played out as depicted above. This epiphany occurs typically when there are consequences at home for getting in trouble in school or other natural or logical consequences.

Unfortunately, more often than not, the students we are talking about are the ones who will not have the support system at home that supports the school. So, while we do get that break from the problem student, we are not helping the student resolve the real issue at hand so that these incidents can lessen or end altogether. If they are not present in class, they cannot learn.

What do we do with the kid who is disruptive in class? Sometimes we must face the fact that we cannot save everyone. Unfortunately, some students may need a different learning environment and should be removed altogether. Saving one student at the cost of twenty-four others is not a sound practice.

Too many instructors give up on the disruptive student(s) too quickly because it is the easier and less time-consuming approach. We must, however, make as many attempts as we can to curb the student's behaviors. I will never advocate giving up on a child. Only after we have exhausted all possibilities will I suggest such a change in educational setting. Sometimes removing a student permanently will work best for the student and his/her classmates. I realize that requesting a student be removed from our classroom setting is not always an option for all of us. But when it is available and necessary, I recommend making the request.

When you have a disruptive student, be sure to follow the school policies. If that means the student gets detention, in-school suspension, or out-of-school suspension, then so be it. But what can you do to make sure the same behaviors are not exhibited all over again?

Here is the good news—we can curb this child's tendency to misbehave. Here is the bad news—it takes extra time on our part, it may take a long time to see the changes taking place in the child, and it may not happen at all. Modeling the appropriate behaviors we wish to see by being our best selves is the first step, as I advocated previously. But what else can we do?

We can raise their self-worth with *The Coaching Classroom* techniques.

The most difficulty I have ever had in reaching a student is when the kid was heavily involved in drugs. We may help inspire that child to seek help, but oftentimes, the drugs will win. That is why it is so important that we inspire them before they turn to drugs. Again, not always a possibility, but definitely a goal we should aspire to achieve.

Whenever we can foster a classroom environment that teaches self-love and respect, we help students make better decisions about how to handle adverse situations they face—one of those being the choice to use and/or abuse drugs and alcohol. There is a strong link between low self-worth and a student's tendency to abuse drugs and alcohol. Negative comments harm a student's self-esteem and often leave them feeling insecure, uncertain of themselves, and confused. These feelings, in turn, are the breeding ground for substance abuse.

Our lessons may be spot-on, but if students are disruptive or on drugs and abusing alcohol, how can they learn in our classrooms? The curriculum is important, but to get the most out of it, we must spend some of that time addressing these other issues or taking preventative measures to keep students from making bad choices that will prohibit them from learning or, moreover, ruining their lives.

So, just how much extra time will it take to curb negative behaviors? I realize we are stretched too thin already. Paperwork threatens to bury us on a daily basis. How about all those online training sessions? To ask you to give even five more minutes when finding time to use the restroom during the day is often a feat in and of itself seems unfair and impossible.

The truth is, if we think about it, nothing that is in our best interest or the best interest of others fails to take up a little extra time and effort on our behalf. It takes time and extra effort to exercise, meditate, clean our homes, take care of our cars, eat right, spend time with family and friends, and so forth. But, when we do it, we know it is worth it. So, as school personnel who have decided to do this job, if there is something we can do to make it better, shouldn't we find the time to do it? The answer is yes.

First, we must determine why the student is being disruptive. And since each student is different, I can offer possible solutions, but to give a script to use on all of them that is guaranteed to be 100-percent effective is not even remotely possible.

It will also depend on your personality and approach to dealing with students. If I give you an idea and implementing it feels awkward or uncomfortable for you, that is exactly how the approach will come off to the students, and you will be left feeling frustrated and decide that this stuff doesn't work. However, there are times when stepping out of our comfort zone and trying something new feels awkward just because it is new and different. Maybe you will need to make an attempt just to see if it is giving you the jitters because it is so new. Maybe you will need to give it some time to see if it begins to work as you get more comfortable with it. You will then likely decide if it is something you need to tweak a bit or eliminate from your repertoire.

Remember, a student who has more serious issues at hand may need to be removed from the classroom or may need to be referred to the guidance counselor or a student assistance program. We must look at the student's behavior and determine if we can help the student ourselves or if the student needs more help than *The Coaching Classroom* setting can offer.

Students on drugs and/or abusing alcohol, who are dealing with other mental health issues, and so on, need more than we can give them. Further, we are not trying to replace personnel or agencies trained to help these students. We are simply trying to incorporate some methods in our classroom that will help students learn, feel better about themselves, and therefore make better choices.

Once we determine that the student does not need outside assistance, we are ready to help that child in our classrooms. Here is what we can do: We must change our behavior toward that student. That is right. I said it before, and I will say it again—we change the student by changing ourselves. We model the behaviors we desire by treating the student the way we want to be treated, and we learn how to "love the unlovable." Remember, these types of students more than any other need our nurturing not our disapproval.

When I was complaining during one of my life coaching classes about how it drove me crazy that my husband made piles of papers and other items and left them sitting out all over the house, my instructor told me that I needed to stop nagging him about it. The first thing I wanted to do was get defensive and ask her why she was on *his* side. It's my house too. Since I was the one who cleaned the house, I had to move all the piles before I could clean. It wasn't fair!

But, before I could unleash on her, as she anticipated my negative reaction to her statement, she countered with the fact that the only way I could change him was to change myself. She suggested I start focusing and complimenting him on what he was doing right.

He mowed the lawn, took care of the cars, emptied the trash, and cleaned up the plates after dinner—he did help out a lot around the house. But then I started to feel resentment building up because no one was thanking me for cooking and cleaning, doing all the laundry and ironing, and so forth. Why did I have to tell him how wonderful he was when no one was doing the same for me?

She explained that I could be right or I could be happy. I thought about it. I have to admit, it was difficult to push down my ego and thank my husband for cleaning up the dishes after I cooked when no one uttered a word of gratitude to me, but I started doing it.

The more I thanked and praised him, the more he started to do around the house. Before long, the piles were put away, and I was receiving gratitude for what I was doing at home as well. It was such a win-win situation and made my house a much happier place.

It works the same way in the classroom. If you are always telling the problem student what he/she is doing wrong, try finding something the student does right. As a matter of fact, you don't have to practice this concept only with the student who gives you grief. It is a good idea to make this concept a habit with all your students.

As I mentioned before, we have eighty-minute class periods (block scheduling). The kids are sometimes hungry when they come to class, and those long class periods can challenge even the most dedicated student to stay on task.

I had a kid come up to me and ask if he could eat a snack during class, and I responded, "Yes, you may, and thank you so much for asking first." I made sure to say this loudly so that his classmates could hear my answer. As a result, my students are better than most in checking with me first to see if they can have a snack rather than sneaking it in like they do in other instructors' classes.

There are times I tell the student no, and the student doesn't argue because I also say, "I am so sorry, but I cannot let you eat right now because…" and then I explain what we are doing that does allow for him/her to eat the snack. "Maybe if we finish before class is over you will have time to eat your snack. Does that sound fair? Thanks for checking with me instead of simply doing it."

Even though I told the student no, I was respectful in doing so, tried to come up with a solution so that the student might be able to have the snack, and thanked the student for asking me for permission.

Does it always work? Oh, my, no, but it works a lot better and more often than not doing it. And, we cannot expect to be respected by a student when we are not being respectful to the student in return.

There are days where I just simply run out of nice and just say, "No, you cannot have a snack today." Yes, I have responded that way to the students, but when they fire back at me or eat the snacks anyway, I simply need to recognize that I got the attitude I gave.

At the same time, if I were nice about it, and the student was still rude and disrespectful, I would feel that the student was more deserving of the punishment that he or she would receive. We know that not every student will respond well to us even if we are being kind when addressing him or her.

I will say it again—students are incredibly perceptive. If we are sitting in our class all day dreading fourth period because we know that problem student is in that class and we don't feel like dealing with him/her today, the students will feel it. We have all looked at a person's expression or walked into a room and felt the negativity oozing off the people we just encountered. They may offer a smile, but we still know, deep down, that they are not pleased to see us.

It is oftentimes very hard to not feel that way about a student who challenges you all the time, but again, we must focus on the positives and change our attitude to help alter the student's behavior. It may take time, but perseverance is the key.

A friend of mine who is a pastor, certified aromatherapist, certified massage therapist, and healer shared a video with me about schools in Finland. According to the video schools in Finland were considered some of the worst-performing schools in the world and now are at the top.

And, while there were other factors that have contributed to this reversal, one part of their newfound success is that they spend less time in the classroom than other countries. Less time, more success.

Did you ever hear the saying, "You cannot get blood from a turnip?" Maybe it is one of those quaint Pennsylvania proverbs, but the point is clear. People only have so much energy and attention to give in any given amount of time. We can require that they come to work or school, but what kind of quality work are we getting from them?

The former co-founder and editor-in-chief of *The Huffington Post* learned this lesson the hard way. Arianna Huffington thought that success meant money, and to obtain it she would need to work long hours and sleep very little. When she literally crashed and burned by falling asleep at her desk, breaking her cheekbone and getting a nasty gash over her eye, she realized that she was not on the right path. She realized that there was more to success than money, but she also extended that philosophy to her staff in the office.

She came to this conclusion by observing her employees. When they really needed to recharge, they instead filled themselves with caffeine and pushed forward, yet they were not actually productive. She set up nap areas in the office where employees can catch those twenty minutes of rest and then continue on with their work. She believes they are more productive when they take that twenty-minute rest in lieu of chugging a beverage that is meant to keep them awake.

No, I am not suggesting that we model kindergarten and institute nap time with milk and cookies in all grade levels. As nice as that sounds to me, I just don't see any school board around the nation going for that proposed plan of action. In mentioning how Arianna Huffington handled the issue at her office, I am simply reaffirming the idea of quality over quantity. Huffington would rather her employees take that twenty-minute break and come back ready to work and be more productive than micromanaging every second while they are on the job.

Think about that concept and ask yourself if you want your students to do some work in forty minutes or quality work in thirty. The truth is, the more you incorporate life coaching into the classroom setting, the better you will be able to get through the required curriculum. The only major problem with incorporating life coaching in the classroom is if you do not have the administrative support to do it.

When you do not have support from your supervisors, it may make being and remaining positive at work a very challenging proposition. But, poor administration is all the more reason for us to keep a positive mindset. We need to incorporate positivity in that environment even more when we have poor administration—for ourselves, our students, and our colleagues. I like to think about how Harry Potter must recall his happiest memory to help create a patronus meant to protect him, and possibly others, from the dementors. These creatures make the people they attack feel like they will never be happy again as they slowly suck the life, and thus their soul, from them. There is truth in that fictional text.

Find that happy place in your mind and create your own patronus when the dementors lurk near you. As I was describing the dementors, I am certain a few faces appeared in your mind's eye. Use your positivity to ward off their soul-sucking negativity.

Now, if you are not allowed to stray from the curriculum to incorporate these techniques, then by all means do not coach yourself out of a job. Administrators will come and go, so if you can tough it out, I encourage you to do so.

If the situation is entirely too toxic for you, you must make a decision about leaving. Please consider all aspects of your employment before you make this choice, as leaving a job can have negative consequences for your mindset as well.

Remember how I told you we spend eighty-six thousand hours of our lives at work? That is a lot of time to be in a toxic environment.

I have had a number of poor administrators over the course of my twenty-nine-year career, and I can tell you that looking back, it was a blessing. At the time I thought I was going to lose my mind, but now I see that I learned more from them about what I did not want to be or become than I could have ever learned if everything had run smoothly.

While I wish I never would have had to work for those individuals, toughing it out and taking away something valuable from the situation served me better than leaving. I made the choice to find the lesson in a bad situation and remain where I was.

If, like me, you elect to stay in your position while under poor leadership, being in a good mood and being kind *in spite* of the people in charge is your best defense and protection against that negativity. Believe me.

I wish I had known then what I know now as I endured years of poor leadership. The frustration, anger, and depression I experienced working under many of them for so many years took a toll on me. I also didn't realize that by allowing them to impact who I was professionally, it affected me personally as well.

I also didn't comprehend that by being upset and angry, I was giving them more power over me. They already had the power of being in charge of me at work, but I let them control so much more of me.

Why did I let them hold so much sway over my mood? Wouldn't I have been so much happier at work, and outside of work, if I had just known and put into practice that simple concept of *choosing* to be happy, no matter what? I know now I would have been better off, and when you know better, you do better.

The same is true with students and colleagues. If we allow that one student to push our buttons or that certain colleague to dictate our mood for the day, we have just relinquished our power to them. And why? Are they worth our joy? The answer is absolutely not. Getting in the right mindset for work helps us keep our power instead of giving it away.

I am not saying that our administration, students, and colleagues won't still make us grind and gnash our teeth, but we now know some ways to keep it from impacting us. How we choose to respond to what others do will be on us.

Remember, we are modeling the behavior we wish to receive back from others. While that does not always work, most of the time, if these people know they cannot get a rise out of us, they will move on to someone else and leave us alone. If we are going to do our job and live our life, isn't it better to do our best and be happy? Let's not waste our time and energy giving someone else power over us.

If you do have an administration who will support *The Coaching Classroom*, reassure them that the time you spend away from the curriculum is invaluable in helping students excel in life. It will actually help them academically and it may cut down on disciplinary measures. If that is not enough, refer to the data in the final chapter to help you convince them of the merits of creating a coaching classroom.

CHAPTER 4

How Do I Change?

A Step-By-Step Guide to Making
Positive Change—and Sticking to It!

Change, as I stated earlier, especially when we are changing ourselves after what has often been years of forming habits, is one of the most challenging tasks we will ever have to attempt. It is not without setbacks and struggle. It will require us to remember what we tell our students about being lifelong learners.

According to Napoleon Hill, from his famous text, *Think and Grow Rich*, "Successful men, in all callings, never stop acquiring specialized knowledge related to their major purpose, business, or profession." Think about that statement. Acquiring specialized knowledge related to our profession demands that we continue learning and trying new practices. And yet, how many teachers do what they have done the same way they have always done it?

As I said before, our life is not meant to be spent simply going through the motions of mediocrity. We are meant for fulfillment. We are meant to make a difference.

My great uncle passed away when he was in his nineties. He was a math teacher and went on to become a principal and pastor in a small town in rural Pennsylvania with a population of roughly seven hundred people, with one traffic light, where he spent his whole life.

I went to his funeral service. Several former students attended and spoke about what a difference he made in their lives. These students had to have been in their fifties and sixties. One came from a long distance to be there, as he no longer lived in that area.

My aunt and uncle had a large, beautiful, well-maintained home on Main Street. No one mentioned the house at the funeral, or how much money they had saved, or their car or clothing, or how handsome my uncle was or wasn't. They spoke of how he made them feel and what a difference he made in their lives.

While aspiring to have a nice home, save money, drive nice cars, and look our best is all well and good and certainly noteworthy, it has nothing to do with our purpose here on earth. Maya Angelou, my favorite poet, once stated, "People will forget what you said, people will forget what you did, but people will never forget how you made them feel."

There is a certain irony in that statement. Oftentimes what we say and do is tied to how we make people feel. So, our reactions as well as our actions are equally important to how others see us.

As morbid as this next question may be, it will help you reflect on whether it is time to take that risk and make a change in yourself and in your classroom setting. If you died tomorrow and your students were asked to each come up and say something nice about how you made them feel, could they do it?

It is not our job to make students like us or to be their friends, and sometimes students simply won't like us because we are doing our jobs. I have students who dislike me for asking them to put their phones away, to sit up, to do their work. There are situations like those where you are not the issue; the student is the issue.

Here I am, talking about the overall message from most of your students. Would they be able to say you cared, that you really wanted them to learn, and that you did your best to make them feel like they could accomplish anything?

Trying *The Coaching Classroom* techniques is not going to be a cakewalk. It may feel incredibly unnatural to us and require us to get out of our comfort zone. Most of us are creatures of habit. Changing what we do in our classroom requires a certain risk. However, it is in taking risks that we often find success.

According to an article in *The Huffington Post* entitled, "How Taking Risks Evokes Leadership Success," by Megan Tull, she says, "Without trial and error—and risk-taking—you remain stagnant, predictable, and, ultimately, you will become complacent. Risks are about pushing yourself until you're operating outside of your comfort zone—with good judgment, of course and allowing yourself to take a step that might feel uncomfortable at first. Growing and realizing your full potential requires it."

You will grow and change by using the techniques I provide in this book and by coming up with some of your own. You keep what works and discard what does not. You revisit what you discarded with one group because it may work with a different group of students.

Just like your academic lessons in the classroom—you try to come up with the best method of teaching the material to your students. The same goes for how you make changes to yourself and ultimately to your classroom.

And sometimes, when you step out of the safety of what you believe to be your prescribed role, you will find that taking a risk to try something new often results in some meaningful change in us. I learn as much from a lesson that didn't go well as I do when a lesson comes together perfectly. Sometimes I believe I actually learn more when what I thought was a great lesson doesn't go as planned. In order for that to happen, I have to try something new. Using the same lessons year after year without attempting new things makes us stagnant. Without taking those risks, we do not grow as people and as educators.

While making changes in yourself is key to having a successful coaching classroom, when you start to implement these coaching practices and really immerse yourself into making your classroom environment a positive place of learning, you will continue to learn and grow from it as well.

Change is difficult, and a lot of people may want to resist it because it is the easier, safer route to stay within our comfort zone. If you have been in education long enough, I am also going to guess that you have thought or even said aloud at one point in time that there is nothing you can do to fix what is happening in the classroom.

You said it because you are only one person. The students are coming to you so deficient and with such bad attitudes that you cannot do anything to fix it. Maybe you believe there is an overall lack of support. The educational system itself is broken, so what are you supposed to do?

We have sat through in-services and trainings where so-called professionals, some of whom have not been in classrooms for centuries or ever, come in and tell us how to do a better job. Then, we go back to our classrooms and try a couple of the suggestions (or not), and when they don't seem to work or there is no follow-up with the presenter, we go back to doing what we have always done. It is easier.

And then there is the "how-to" part of changing what has long since become ingrained in us. Much of what we do is what we have always done—even if it is not working for us. This has a lot to do with our subconscious minds, which, as I stated previously, were formed from birth to age seven. So, a great deal of our opinions of the world and how we operate is a part of our minds that we don't even realize is controlling our every move.

That is not to say that we don't create other habits after age seven. We do. But how do we change those habits? Well, to get into our subconscious minds to make a change, we either have to use hypnotherapy, repetition, or undergo an emotional tragic experience.

The worst apps, in my opinion, are hypnosis apps. You have no idea who has made it, if the person is certified, or even if it is being done correctly, for that matter. You should never allow people to do anything with your subconscious mind unless you trust them explicitly and know that they have the credentials to practice hypnosis. If they make one mistake during the hypnotherapy, it could cause a whole avalanche of new issues.

No one I know wants to experience a tragedy so they can change their subconscious mind. A tragedy can cause you to make changes—and you have a 50/50 shot of which way that change will go based on how you process the tragedy. It influences some people to greatness and others to failure.

I like to refer here to the book and movie *Rudy*, written by and based on the life of Daniel "Rudy" Ruettiger. The autobiography came out after the huge success of the movie, and it is after reading the book that I realized that what actually happened is somewhat different from the movie, as Hollywood often does its own thing when a story ends up on the big screen. The overall premise is still the same, though. I will give you the skinny of it for all intents and purposes.

(Spoiler alert!) Rudy is a kid with learning difficulties from a blue-collar family. No one supports his dream of playing football for and graduating from the University of Notre Dame except his best friend. In the movie, upon graduation, Rudy takes a job in the factory where his family and best friend work. One day during lunch, his best friend gives him a Notre Dame jacket. Shortly thereafter, his best friend is killed in front of him in an explosion in the factory.

The next thing that happens is Rudy leaves for Notre Dame. According to the text, there was this voice inside his head telling him, "Leave." He wrote, "All those times Siskel had told me, 'Get out of here. You don't belong here. What good is security if you're not happy?' And this is what it took for me to finally listen?"

It was an emotional tragic experience, and that is how Rudy changed. We don't want anything like that to happen to help us change our habits. While we can certainly go to a hypnotherapist to make changes to our subconscious mind, there is only one positive solution that we can do for ourselves to change our subconscious mindset.

That positive solution occurs through the use of repetition. That is why I tell students, "You are great. You are awesome. You are amazing," every day. That is why they look at their vision boards during class every day. That is how you can change your subconscious mind.

According to a multitude of experts, there are a certain number of set days it takes to create a habit. While they all differ slightly in their opinion, they are rather close in their estimation. What I have been taught is that it takes thirty full days for any change to become a habit. That is thirty days of consistency. Miss one day, and we need to start over.

Beyond that, habits have three components to them. According to the book *The Power of Habit* by Charles Duhigg, "The Golden Rule of Habit Change includes cue, routine, and reward."

Using the same cue and same reward, according to Duhigg, we can change the routine and therefore change a habit. He argues that most habits are not changed because when the temptation to fulfill the habit is aroused (the cue), a new routine must be put in place to replace the old reward. For example, consider the habit of smoking. When the desire to smoke (the cue) comes into play, we must instead replace it with another routine and a reward. That new routine must be established or we most likely will not stick with the idea of giving up smoking.

My dad gave up smoking three and a half packs of Camel cigarettes per day by replacing the urge to smoke with a piece of candy. He gained some weight, but his lungs are intact, and he is eighty-nine years old now. Without the new routine or the reward of the taste of the candy, he most likely would not have been successful in breaking the habit of smoking cigarettes.

Here is the thing about doing what is easier. Earlier, I told you that everything in this lifetime that is worthwhile requires a little more effort on our behalf and some self-discipline. It is easier to overeat and eat all the wrong foods and harder to discipline ourselves to eat less and eat right. It is easier to sit on the couch instead of exercising. It is easier to lie than it is to be truthful to someone. It is easier to tell someone off when we are upset than to say something nice when someone does something right. It is easier to do poorly in school in lieu of studying and making the "A" honor roll.

The truth of the matter is that everything that is better for us requires some self-discipline on our behalf. We have become a very complacent society, doing what is fast and easy. Giving trophies to all players despite whether they have the talent or aptitude for the sport. Having technology that puts items and people only a click away from us has changed us. Placing orders for fast food and already-shopped for, partially prepared items that allow us to "prepare" dinner faster has also changed us. All of these perks, designed to make our lives easier, may only make it easier for us to become okay with not putting in the effort for the more rewarding outcomes.

We are tired, we are overworked, and it can leave us defeated if we let it. But we went into a career where ordinariness is not an option, where we must be willing to hang in there and try new ways to reach our students. We have integrity and won't just put in our time and collect a paycheck, right? So, doing what is easy and requires less effort is not for us.

I am reminded of the story I tell my students entitled, "Three Feet from Gold." The story was first shared with me by my mentor Peggy Caruso from Napoleon Hill's book *Think and Grow Rich*.

There was a man named R. U. Darby, who set out to Colorado from his home in Maryland to mine for gold during the time of the famous Gold Rush. He hastily staked his claim to some land and began to search for gold with his pick and shovel. It took him weeks of hard labor, but he found a shiny piece of ore and set out to get machinery to bring it to surface. He discreetly covered his find and headed home where he told his family and friends about it, asking them to loan him money for the machinery. He returned to the mine and learned that he had found one of the richest in all the state! But, before long, the vein of gold seemed to have disappeared. They searched and searched and found nothing. Darby and his uncle quit drilling, sold the machinery to a junkman, and returned home to pay back his family and friends—which took years. The junkman called in a mining engineer who surveyed the land and determined that the vein picked back up three feet from where Darby and his uncle quit drilling. The junkman went on to make millions.

What does this story teach us? We have heard this line before and may have uttered it ourselves—failure is only defeat if we let it keep us down; if we give up. Many of us do just that. We work and work and work and right before we break through that glass ceiling, we quit. We figure it is not going to happen, it's not meant to be, or we become too discouraged to go on pursuing our goals. The key to making changes is perseverance and not letting anyone else tell us who we are and what we will become.

RULE: #4

Do not give up and resort to what is easy. Change is hard and requires a lifelong commitment.

What if Walt Disney believed that he "lacked imagination and creativity" when he was fired from his newspaper job? What if Oprah Winfrey believed she "wasn't fit for television" when she was not given the position as anchor on the news? What if Michael Jordan believed his coaches when he was cut from his high school basketball team and just gave up the idea of ever playing basketball again?

These people persevered and did not allow others to define them. How many of our students are out there with the cure to cancer but will work at some menial job because one of their family members, some teacher or coach, or their best friend told them they weren't smart enough or good enough, and they believed it?

When the experts looked at Dave Pelzer after the horrific physical and psychological abuse he endured as a child at the hands of his own mother and proclaimed that he would never be "right," Dave says, "I never saw it that way."

When the Miracle Man, Morris Goodman, crashed an airplane, and the doctors said he would be a vegetable, only ever able to simply blink his eyes for the rest of his life, he said, "It didn't matter how they saw me; that is not how I saw myself." Morris saw himself walking out of the hospital by Christmas, and guess what he did? He walked out of the hospital by Christmas. It doesn't matter how others see us; it is how we see ourselves. That is one of many steps that helps us change.

Too many people do not realize they are in charge of their own destiny. I have a wooden sign hanging in my classroom that says, "You are the author of your own life story." There is also a saying by Seth Godin that states, "Instead of wondering when your next vacation is, you ought to set up a life you don't need to escape from."

It is important for us to remember and to remind our students that they are in charge of how their day is going to go, that they are responsible for setting up how they want their lives to turn out. I am not saying they can control everything that happens to them, but they sure can control how they respond to it.

Peggy, my mentor, told me about a day where it seemed that everything that could go wrong did for her. She spent a great deal of time picking out the perfect outfit and curling her hair for an important meeting. She was getting out of her car in the rain, with no coat or umbrella, juggling all these important papers in her hand, along with her morning cup of Joe. She was trying to hurry to get inside.

Instead, she slipped and fell and landed in a muddy puddle. The papers scattered all over the wet pavement, her hair got soaked and went flat, and her clothes were ruined from the rain, mud, and, of course, spilled coffee from the cup she had been holding but ultimately dropped during the fall.

Most of us would cry, swear, ask, "Why me?" and just go home. Not Peggy. She laughed because she knew there was nothing she could do except get up and do her best to put herself back together again. She knew the importance of responding positively to situations such as these instead of letting them ruin her day. She *decided* she was going to have a good day, and so she did despite what happened to her.

How many times have you spilled a drink or food on your clothing, got behind someone who had no concept of reaching the speed limit, needed to print something for class and the printer was broken, or worse yet, discovered your computer wasn't working properly at all? How did you handle it? How do you handle the unruly student, the disgruntled parent? Do you go and complain to your colleagues in the faculty room?

The faculty room is a great place to go if we want to find people who are as miserable as we are. It seems to be a breeding ground for dissension. I used to think it was okay to go in there and vent. Once I got it out of my system, I would be okay and be able to go back to my classroom and smile and continue with my day.

While once every now and again that may be true, what genuinely occurs is that we create the habit of complaining every day and listening to everyone else's complaints as well. The faculty room becomes a place where everyone discusses what is wrong with everything at work. If we cannot change it, we are wasting precious time and energy focusing on what is not working instead of what is working or what we would like to see happen.

Our miracle man Morris Goodman sums up how he beat the odds by saying, "Man becomes what he thinks about." So, if we are thinking about and verbalizing what is wrong, we will get exactly that which has become our focus.

Now don't go thinking you need to sit around focusing on how they need to reinstate corporal punishment because that is what you would like to see happen. That isn't what I meant. Daydreaming about winning the lottery and sitting in the Caribbean sipping on a cool tropical drink listening to Jimmy Buffet isn't exactly what I had in mind either. That scenario may be what you want to happen as well, but that too is not my meaning.

I mean, picture the day going the way you want it to go and/or picture yourself handling all the snafus that come your way in the happiest, most professional way you can imagine. Then, make a decision that you will handle obstacles in that manner.

You may have to avoid the faculty room altogether. After all, sitting in there listening to the complaints, even if you are not contributing to them, is still not good for you. Very few people can subject themselves to that kind of negativity day in and day out and come out of it unscathed.

I don't want you to think that I am saying all faculty room conversations are negative or that the people who frequent the faculty room are all people to avoid. There is positive talk, and there are positive people in the faculty room. You simply need to watch out for the people who seem to go in there just to complain and fire up the troops.

In our faculty room, we will discuss a few issues, not so much to complain but to figure out what is going on with a kid or situation. That is the use of a different approach other than complaining.

We have an instructor at our school who has been teaching since 1971 and would make more money in retirement, but he keeps on teaching year after year. He seems to be one of the few people who doesn't allow negativity to affect him. He is unique.

When you run into that consistent complaining faculty member in the faculty room, or when you encounter a negative individual anywhere, to create a new, positive habit, you will need to turn the conversation around to discuss what is going well. If that doesn't work, you may need to remove yourself from that person or group altogether.

And, time is your ally here. As I said before, it takes thirty days for a habit to form. Thirty days. Seems like a long time when we are trying to lose weight. It took years to gain the ten pounds, but we want it gone in a week. We want our hot food hot and our cold food cold, but we want it in minutes and become irritated when it is not done correctly. We are impatient with what we want. We expect miracles when we think we have put in enough effort and enough of our time.

Our habits did not develop overnight. Spending thirty days to change them and continuing to work on improving is not an unrealistic amount of time to put into making a change—especially when that change is for the better.

We live in a fast-paced society, so this concept of slowing down and having patience may not be part of our repertoire, but thirty days in the grand scheme of things is not that long and, if we focus on what we will gain at the end of the thirty days, it may help keep us motivated.

So, now that we know it will take thirty days to make a change, what else do we need to do? Remember that we are always going to be tempted to slide back into our old habits, so we must revisit the changes.

Napoleon Hill wrote the book *Think and Grow Rich* in 1937. He spent twenty years interviewing five hundred millionaires and compiled his findings in print for the rest of the world to read. By 2015, the book had sold more than one hundred million copies. I heard somewhere that most persons who are successful tout the book as being one to which they attribute to their success. Successful people also compile lists of books to invest in, and *Think and Grow Rich* is considered to be on the list of one of the top eight books to buy. It is said that more millionaires were born from this book than any other text. Did you also know that most will say that they read it over and over again? They do not just read it one time and then put it away for safekeeping.

Have you ever heard of Bob Proctor? Bob Proctor, born in Canada in 1934, is a Canadian-American author, entrepreneur, and motivational speaker who has a net worth of twenty-million dollars. Did you also know that Bob Proctor has allegedly read the book twenty times? Why do you think he has read the same book over and over again? It is most likely because he is revisiting the habits he wants to maintain. He wants to learn something new each time he reads the book, and he knows repetition is also one of the best ways to make positive changes that will stick.

To develop a habit over a thirty-day period, repetition is imperative. For example, if you have a negative self-image, the habit I mentioned earlier in starting your day off right (where you look in the mirror every day for thirty days and tell yourself that you are beautiful/handsome, smart, kind, successful, and so forth) is a good place to start. It is part of the positive self-talk that changes your perspective about yourself. You should do it in the morning and in the evening when you brush your teeth. You can also do it when you use the restroom and are washing your hands afterward. You should keep saying it as many times a day as you can over a thirty-day period. How much more successful in improving your self-worth do you think you will be?

Have you ever watched a television show or movie on television and see the same commercial played several times during the course of your viewing? It is not an accident that the same commercial was shown to you more than once during the time you were watching a show.

How about the commercials that repeat a message or their phone number again and again in those thirty-to-sixty seconds they have your attention? None of what is happening is without design. That repetition is a propaganda technique that is being used to ensnare you. It works for advertisers, and it can work for you as you attempt to make positive changes in yourself.

There is a roughly seventeen-minute-long, black-and-white video called "Validation" on YouTube. The video has a great storyline (despite being so short). This video contains several invaluable lessons, but the most important is how it reminds us how necessary it is to repeatedly provide positive reinforcement to people.

There is concern that doing something too much can make people immune to it. There are people who tell each other they love one another each time they hang up the phone. Because they do it each time, some would argue that it is no longer special to hear it—that saying it out of habit is not a good practice. I see where that argument would have merit.

I cannot be certain that students are looking at their vision boards and spending those three minutes each day visualizing their goals coming to life. They may be quiet but wandering somewhere else in their minds as I ask them to get out their vision boards and put on the music for them. I cannot know if saying, "You are great. You are awesome. You are amazing," is sinking in and helping each of them feel better about themselves.

What I can say is this—setting goals, dedicating quiet time each day to concentrate on those goals, and saying the same positive phrase daily is giving them the tools they may need later as well as doing something that may be benefiting them now. It certainly has no negative effect on the energy in my classroom, and the positive feedback I have received suggests that it is working.

As I said earlier, you are not going to reach every student. But, reaching one right now is better than reaching no one. Giving them these tools is crucial so that when some of them do decide that they want to make positive changes in their lives, they will know what to do.

When I give students those positive affirmations, I look them in the eyes and say it, and I mean it. I know it reaches many. I also know there are some who will not immediately benefit from it.

While I would love to implement all these coaching techniques in the classroom setting and be able to tell you that in doing so I have saved the world, sadly, I cannot. What I can say is that I know that I am making a difference with more students than ever before. Incorporating positive lessons into my classroom has not hurt but instead has improved my classroom environment and me as an educator and person. Due to the fact that I know repetition is effective, I will make this statement yet again—there is no one-size-fits-all for education. However, any attempt at empowering students to make the choice to do something worthwhile instead of harmful should be our goal.

Teaching them the power of using visualization to escape bad situations instead of turning to drugs and alcohol is empowering our students. Teaching them that they have a purpose, letting them know they matter and that we are glad they are here, helps their self-worth so that they do not abuse their bodies with drugs and alcohol or, in some cases, cutting. Improving their self-worth can also help with depression and possibly help prevent a suicide. Changing our own attitudes and practices in our classrooms and in our lives makes positive changes for our students and anyone else around us.

I finally relented and joined Facebook in 2008. My best friend, Amy Phillips Nunez, pestered me to join so that we could stay in touch easier since I live in Pennsylvania and she lives in Florida.

A few years after being on there I had acquired a rather large friend list. One day, I received a message from a kid I knew in high school. He thanked me for being nice to him and told me that he had thought about killing himself back then, but that the smile I gave him every day kept him from doing it.

My smile. Something so simple that we often take for granted. We do not always know whom we reach until much later, if ever, but we still must work to try to make those positive changes.

I have a sign hanging on a corkboard near my computer. While I have changed out everything else on that corkboard year after year, this saying is the one item I have hung up in my room since I started teaching back in January of 1992. It is by Haim Ginott, and it says,

"I have come to a frightening conclusion. I am the decisive element in the classroom. It is my personal approach that creates the climate. It is my daily mood that makes the weather. As a teacher, I possess tremendous power.... To make a child's life miserable or joyous. I can humiliate or humor, hurt or heal.

In all situations, it is my response that decides whether a crisis will be escalated or de-escalated, and a child humanized or dehumanized."

Like it or not, that quote is true. We set the climate for our classrooms with our own demeanor. I am not suggesting we ride around the room on a tricycle wearing a big red nose and toss candy at our students. But if we want to see change in our classroom, we must first be the change.

As we know from the faculty room, misery loves company. Sometimes you will be challenged more by your own family, friends, colleagues, students, etc. when you are in a good mood. Your colleagues will miss the person who complained with them and will do and say things to try to drag you down. Your students may not know how to deal with kindness and may try to get you to be mean to them because that is what they know and is therefore their comfort zone.

I will still have my moments, but when the students try to push my buttons and I remain calm and happy, I see them slowly realizing that there may be another way to respond to situations. Initially, these students may be angry that they are not making me respond the way they are pushing me to respond, but after a while, they will break down. I can see them almost studying me, trying to figure me out. As you begin to incorporate these techniques, you may see the same kind of situation occur in your classroom.

We must remind ourselves time and time again that we can only control what we can control, and that is us. Making positive changes allowed me to be a better wife and mother, meet the right friends, enjoy time with colleagues at work, and show my students that there is another way to be. And you know what? We are all better because of it.

CHAPTER 5

I Am Changing. What Else Do I Need to Do?

*Sharing Positive Change in Yourself and
Others So Your Students Can Relate*

Once you begin to make the transformation in yourself, you need to find assignments that incorporate life coaching techniques in the classroom setting.

We have discussed the use of feng shui, having positive quotes painted onto the walls, and surrounding yourself in your classroom or office with what makes you smile. We already talked about having students write down their goals and then make vision boards that they spend time looking at on a daily basis.

Setting goals and getting students thinking with success principles puts them on the right track to obtaining their goals.

The students set their goals and then create visual representations of their goals with a vision board. As students work on their vision boards, I show them sample vision boards that I look up on Google Images. There are also YouTube videos of famous people who have made and used vision boards that you may wish to show them.

I mentioned in passing that I used the technique of having students listen to music while looking at their vision boards. YouTube is a fantastic source. You can find just about any type of music on there from melodies to help you study to tunes that help remove subconscious blocks.

Does it work? I cannot say that it does or it doesn't, but I know this much—playing music that may help students cannot hurt. So, I select different songs to use for their quiet time with their vision boards. I play the music softly so that it is background noise and not disruptive. The time that elapses helps me keep track of the time that has passed too, so the music serves as a stopwatch. When the music stops, they know they are done. I also make it a point to say, "Good job. Thank you," when I end the music.

Are you familiar with the law of attraction? It is a concept meaning, in the simplest of terms, we attract to us that which becomes our focus. Did you ever think about a friend you hadn't talked to in a very long time only for that friend to call you or to have her name come up in conversation with someone else? Some would argue that this is an example of the law of attraction at work.

This next visual tool I use in the classroom is based on the idea of using the law of attraction. It also coincides with the idea of setting goals and pursuing them. I have students write themselves a check using a printed blank check I found royalty-free on Google Images. They are slightly larger than a regular check, and I have them printed on cardstock. Many of the students opt to put them on their vision boards.

The idea is for the students to set a financial goal to achieve and then write a check to themselves for the amount of money they wish to obtain. It is dated using the date they determined is their deadline for achieving the goal, and they sign it by the individual who will be writing them the check. If they are not certain who will issue the check to them, they may scribble a signature or leave it blank. This idea is not an original one I came up with. I read the book and watched the movie *The Secret*.

Jack Canfield, author of the *Chicken Soup for the Soul* series and several other successful books, stars in the film *The Secret*. He talks about how he used the law of attraction in a similar way as I was with my students. Mr. Canfield did not use a blank check but instead changed a regular one-dollar bill into a $100,000 bill that he stuck to his ceiling. He placed it there so it was the last thing he saw when he went to sleep and the first thing he saw each morning.

Jack Canfield met W. Clement Stone, who taught him about the law of attraction. He suggested that Mr. Canfield set a goal so lofty that he would know that it was the law of attraction working if it were to come to fruition.

He visualized his goal on a daily basis as if it already happened. Nothing happened for the first thirty days. Then, he thought about this book he had already written, and he realized that if he sold four hundred thousand copies for $.25 each, he would reach his financial goal.

He then went to a store and saw *The National Enquirer* on a newsstand and realized that getting his book advertised there would draw the audience for it.

He went to do a speaking engagement, and afterward, a woman came up to him and told him she really enjoyed his presentation. She wanted to meet to talk to him some more. When he asked whom she worked for, she stated, "I am a freelancer, but I sell most of my stuff to *The National Enquirer.*"

So, amid *The Twilight Zone* music going off in his head, he realized everything had come full circle. He made roughly $92,000 that year—$8,000 short of the bill he altered—but was he disappointed or of the belief this kind of thing does not work? Not in the least. His wife encouraged him to write himself a check for a million dollars as his following year's financial goal since he did that with his $100,000-goal and came so close to achieving it. His publisher ended up writing him a check that next year for, you guessed it, one million dollars.

The law of attraction only works when we do. Jack Canfield didn't set a financial goal and then grab a bag of Doritos and spend all his time on the couch watching Netflix. The bill on the ceiling sparked his thought processes and was followed up by action.

Which brings me to the next part of my classroom practices that have been effective—gratitude. The same techniques that helped us make a change within can be shared with others.

When a student does something I deem acceptable for the classroom environment, I acknowledge it. Most of us do. That is an easy one. I know most teachers already incorporate gratitude into the classroom environment, but a reminder, as well as telling you some of the ways I use it, might help you to use it more often.

I was shocked by the increase in gratitude and kind statements in my classroom from my students when I began to tell them, "You are great. You are awesome. You are amazing." Many of them say, "Thank you," or, "You are too," in response. Again, modeling the positive behaviors is key.

RULE #5

Once you are in a good place yourself, the positivity you model will help make the positive exercises in your classroom a greater success.

In addition to making positive statements to my students on a daily basis, I have positive quotes that I keep in a jar on a table at the front of my classroom. Students may take a positive quote out of the jar anytime they wish, but every Friday, I go around the room and hand them out to my students to help them get in the right frame of mind for the weekend. It's ironic to think that being away from school is not a good thing for many students.

When I was growing up, I was fortunate enough to love going home after school and being home on the weekends, holidays, and during the summer. For too many students, spending time away from school requires that they spend time in environments that are not safe, relaxing, or positive. To help them prepare for it, I offer positive quotes. Not every student takes one, but most do, and some take one from the jar every day they have class.

I have been told that many of my students have kept every single one of the quotes they got from my class. I was told that one of my students taped the quotes to his wall in his bedroom at home so he could read them and keep himself in a positive mindset. Again, something so simple that takes a little extra time on our part makes such a huge impact on many of our students.

We can also use positivity quotes to curb undesirable behaviors. If a student says something unacceptable in class, we can ask them to write a positive quote for the jar that is an antonym for what the student just said that was negative.

This use of the jar incorporates the idea of positivity, and by having the student write a quote that is an antonym of it, the concept also incorporates English Language Arts Common Core standards. Win-win!

The same goes for sticky notes. I put positive phrases on colored sticky notes and have them hanging on a cabinet just inside the door to my classroom. The notes have a range of phrases on them from, "You matter," to, "Hang in there," to, "You are meant to be here."

Students may take a sticky note anytime they need a word of encouragement. The idea is that they can stick it on their notebook, binder, or book that they carry. They can look at it and read it all day long. The note provides the students with a visual tool to help them stay in a positive mindset.

I was shocked last school year when one of our most popular, cool boys came to my desk and said, "We are allowed to have those sticky notes, right?" I told him yes, and he walked up while the class was working on an assignment and took one in front of all his classmates.

He didn't try to grab one while no one was looking. He wasn't embarrassed. The fact that he went up and took one of those sticky notes during class was as good for him as it was for his classmates since he is viewed by others as a kid to emulate.

Did you ever read the statistics that state that people only remember 20 percent of what you say and 80 percent of what they say themselves? I put that concept to use one year with gratitude notebooks.

I gave each student a notebook, and the student would write each day, "I am so happy and grateful that I passed my Keystone Literature exam with a proficient or advanced score in the spring of (whatever year we were going into at that time)."

Then, the student would have to write one adjective to compliment himself/herself: "I am smart," or, "I am talented," or, "I am handsome," and so forth.

I actually collected the notebooks and graded them as part of their participation grade. The idea was that the repetitive nature of saying the student would pass the exam would help them believe they could pass it. And, by having students write it themselves, it would become ingrained in their minds.

Having them compliment themselves served to help turn their negative opinions of themselves into more positive ones. Also, asking students to use adjectives supports my curriculum as well.

I would love to include all the links to videos on YouTube that I have used to inspire my students, but they become obsolete or broken so quickly I fear my list would be useless in a short period of time. So, I will simply describe to you what I use and hope you will be able to find it and discover some good ones on your own.

The first one I use is Susan Boyle's first audition on *Britain's Got Talent*. I use that video when I want to emphasize the importance of not allowing others' judgment of you to influence who you are or become. It is also a good lesson about judging people by appearance and pursuing your dreams no matter your age. Susan Boyle was forty-seven years old in that video.

Another favorite is the seventeen-minute, black-and-white "Validation" video that I mentioned earlier as my inspiration for saying, "You are great. You are awesome. You are amazing," to my students. It shows the two meanings of validation—one for validating parking and the other for receiving validation from another person. This one is great, but also shows you how dangerous it is to only feel good when another person tells you that you are great. I show this video and then start my daily affirmations afterward.

And, like asking students to write an adjective about themselves directly linked *The Coaching Classroom* technique to my core curriculum, we are able to use the "Validation" video to discuss multiple-meaning words in English.

There are also great movie clips that inspire students. I have used several from the movie *Rudy,* and most are available on YouTube. Other clips I use include scenes called "Finding the Joy" and "Final Scene" from the movie *The Bucket List.* These clips from the movie *The Bucket List* were also located on YouTube.

I also use various clips from the movie *The Pursuit of Happyness* and from the book and film called *The Secret.* This book and film, as I mentioned earlier, deal with the law of attraction.

I use more than Jack Canfield's story on *The Secret.* I do use several other parts of *The Secret* in my classroom, much of which is available on YouTube. I find one of my favorite clips from the movie on YouTube by typing in "The Secret guy who crashes a plane." The story is about Morris Goodman, who survived a plane crash and used the power of his mind to defy the odds and heal himself. I mentioned him earlier in Chapter 4 when I talked about how it does not matter how others see you, but how you see yourself.

I also talked earlier about the use of music. There are music titles on YouTube that suggest that listening to them helps manage stress. We will listen to that music during vision board time, but it can be used at other times during class as well, such as when students are working independently. I also use songs in the classroom with positive lyrics. I play "Brave" by Sara Bareilles, "Stronger (What Doesn't Kill You)" by Kelly Clarkson, "Hall of Fame" by The Script, "Don't Stop Believin'" by Journey, and "Smile" by Nat King Cole. Sometimes I play the songs and put the lyrics up on the television screen so students can both see and hear the positive messages.

Something I tried a few years ago and continue to do today that really caught on was music in the hallway on Fridays. I participated in a walk for suicide prevention and awareness at the very beginning of September a few years back. At the walk, they had numerous tables where volunteers were handing out stickers, bracelets, pencils, and magnets with a crisis intervention phone number, along with other miscellaneous items.

I told them I was a teacher and asked if they would be willing to give me items to distribute to my students. They gave me hundreds. So, I talked to the other two teachers who shared the hallway with me and asked if they wanted to play uplifting music and hand these items out with me.

They agreed, and so for the entire month of September, we played songs such as "I Will Survive" by Gloria Gaynor, "Don't Stop Believin'" by Journey, and the "1-800" song by Logic while handing out these items to students between classes.

When October rolled around, students coming down our hallway kept asking us, "Where's the music?" So, we made it a Friday tradition.

Sometimes we hand out treats, sometimes stickers, sometimes erasers, pencil sharpeners, pencils, and so forth. We try to pick a variety of music to appeal to everyone's tastes, but we also try to come up with themes.

For example, National Peepers Day is March 16th, so we played the song, "Jump" by Van Halen and handed out gummy frogs to the kids. At other times, we just sing and dance and make fools out of ourselves for them, and we will dress the part for some of the music.

We played "What Ifs" by Kane Brown and made sure we wore our cowboy hats that day. We played "Ice Ice Baby" by Vanilla Ice and wore sunglasses and rapped the song for them. Silly, but worth it because they loved it.

I read from a variety of books. As you may have guessed, a lot of the information I use comes from Dave Pelzer's book *Help Yourself*. A great deal of my other material comes from Napoleon Hill's *Think and Grow Rich*. I told you the story from this book entitled "Three Feet from Gold." I have also used the story about the fly and "Burn the Ships."

The story about the fly is the premise that the insect will keep going in the same direction, flying into the window over and over, and we will most likely find his little corpse lying there when he expires. However, if the fly would have just turned his focus elsewhere, he would have seen the open door that would lead him outside. If what we are doing isn't working, we need to change our focus and direction.

The story about burning the ships is one you may have heard before. There is debate about the truth of it, but it is a lesson from Cortes in 1519. The premise was that his men were outnumbered and had little chance of winning, so when they got to shore he ordered them to burn the ships. That way his men had to win or die. There was no safety net to save them if they failed. They had no choice except to win—and they did.

I have also had guest speakers come in and talk with my students. Actually, that is how I first met my mentor and life coach instructor, Peggy Caruso. I have a firm belief that everything happens for a reason. I believe that even our encounters with others are not just a matter of chance, but part of our designed destiny.

About fifteen years into my career, the administration at our school changed drastically. At the time, I hadn't begun to work on myself and therefore was not what I would consider to be a model employee. Looking back, there were areas of improvement that I needed work on to grow both personally and professionally.

I told you earlier that our previous administration was less than favorable and that it was the best lesson I ever had. Here is how having poor administration helped me in the long run.

When the administration changed, we got two people in authority positions who would ask for our opinions but really didn't want them. I gave my opinion when they asked for it, and sometimes when they didn't ask for it, and as a result, I was not their favorite person.

I am very passionate about the students, school, and community where I work. We all know people who come to a school to use it as a stepping stone to advance their careers or who go into administration as a means of bolstering their retirement income, but their hearts do not appear to be in their job. Their decisions end up being more about what is easier for them than what is best for the students, the school, and the community. Unfortunately, these two administrators seemed to fit that description. It was difficult to sit back silently and watch it all unfold. So, I wasn't silent, and because I hadn't worked on myself yet, my method of expressing myself was not productive.

You will never agree with every boss you ever have—I think our current administration does a great job, and we still disagree at times—but I believe that if the boss cares about the students, you can tolerate decisions that you don't always think are the best. At any rate, during the eight years I endured this subpar leadership, I allowed myself to be miserable. Remember, that is a choice, and because I didn't know better, I allowed their poor leadership to impact how I felt.

There were times I really didn't think my career was going to survive while I was under their charge, but I never gave up on my students. I still tried to find the best way to reach them, and I decided it would be through positive reinforcement. I read up on it and clumsily went about implementing positive reinforcement with my lessons.

Then, one morning, while I was getting ready for work, I heard this advertisement on the local radio station about a new life coaching business opening up in my town of residence. The ad caught my attention, and I called the owner. She told me what she did, and it was exactly what I had been trying to do in my classroom.

She offered to be a guest speaker for my students. I was thrilled. She came in and did a fantastic job. We talked some more. She told me she was offering a life coaching class, and I signed up.

During the year that I took the course with Peggy, I soon learned that I had a whole lot of work to do on myself. Ironically, I thought I was there to simply learn how to help my students, but by working on myself, I, in turn, was better equipped to help those in my classroom.

I even learned to look back on the negative experience with my former administration with gratitude. As I said, while I still do not condone the way they treated me, I know that through adversity comes some of our most valuable lessons.

After listening to a talk show on the radio during which a person told of his life's journey from despair to success, my son, who was in the car with me listening to the program, asked, "Did you ever notice that most people with success stories have had some really bad experiences first?"

In many ways, he is right. When we are comfortable, we are often content and not eager to make any changes. We settle where we are and feel we are doing "good enough." A bad experience either makes people wallow in despair for the rest of their lives, or they use it to inspire them to make a change.

There was a commercial that a number of famous athletes appeared in during which they were discussing how to be a success. Their answer was "defeat." The defeat didn't make them quit. It made them who they are today. That concept is often the opposite of what we think of when we think of someone who was defeated. We see a quitter. The athletes used it as inspiration.

My experience with my previous administration was the best thing that could have happened to me. At the time, while I was going through it and lacked the knowledge that I could learn from it, I was in the throes of despair.

Today, I am grateful. We often look at negative moments in our lives and feel sorry for ourselves. No one relishes the idea of being faced with negative circumstances, but without those negative events, I would not be who I am today. What I learned during that difficult time in my life has been invaluable. I use that experience to inspire my students to hang in there and to ask themselves what they should learn from what is happening to them. As I said, everything happens for a reason.

We are also lucky enough to have another talented individual in our community. Our local author Krissy Gasbarre came in and spoke with students about writing her latest books *Etched in Sand* and *Raising Ryland*. She co-authored *Etched in Sand* with Regina Calcaterra.

The story is a true account about Sandra and her siblings and the abusive environment where she grew up in Long Island, New Jersey. Ms. Gasberre also co-authored a book about the rewards and challenges associated with raising a transgender child in another book, *Raising Ryland*.

Her novels deal with topics that impact so many teens today. I had all my students attend this presentation, and I believe discussing these two topics with my students helped them learn that they are not alone.

I was also fortunate enough to have the Warren Ryan Fearless Speaking Academy come in and speak with my students a few years ago now. Although this group is no longer together, the presentation they offered to my students was phenomenal. I offered this presentation to all grade levels and allowed students to sign-up to attend.

There are times I elect to make attendance at these types of presentations mandatory and times when I make them optional. This presentation was an optional one. I simply use my gut to determine how to handle attendance at guest presentations.

A small group of about forty students opted to attend. The FSA group members came in and talked to students about being their personal best.

Then, later that evening, the group was doing a presentation at our local theater. All my students were invited to attend the free presentation that evening at the Reitz Theater.

My son and I went there after his basketball game, and there sat one of my students. Yes, only one, but here is what you need to know. He had to drive or get a ride to travel the forty-mile distance to the theater to hear them speak. His home situation is difficult at best. And yet he was there, listening to a positive message and being inspired. Again, even if you only reach one kid, it is worth it.

One year, I had a group of students that I ended up teaching for two years in a row. Our school started out as a sophomore through senior school. Once freshmen were moved to the high school setting in all the surrounding school districts, we pushed to have freshmen attend our school as well.

Our school is a comprehensive, vocational-technical school that teaches students their academic courses and their Career and Technical programs all in one building. Currently, there are four different school districts bussed to our school daily for a full day of instruction.

Although we like to believe that students come to us for all the right reasons, sometimes students make decisions about their education based on friendships or boyfriends and girlfriends rather than what is best for them and their future.

So, they would go to the middle school for three years, go to the high school for their freshman year, and then have to make the decision to leave their new school to come to our school if they wished to enroll in one of our CTE programs. Oftentimes, students would not transfer because they didn't want to change schools again or leave new friends or a boyfriend or girlfriend. By changing our school to grades nine through twelve, it allowed students to go from middle school to our school directly or to high school—a much easier transition.

While most of my career was spent teaching sophomores, I opted to teach the freshmen when they first came to our school. I liked the idea of being the first instructor they had when they arrived so I could set the tone. A new principal came in and switched me back to sophomores. So, the group I had their freshman year also had me their sophomore year. I wasn't sure how that would play out.

Well, we ended up really bonding. They actually asked me to loop with them like the teacher did in the book/movie, *Freedom Writers.* While I loved the idea, I also thought they would miss out on what our junior and senior English instructors could share with them, so I didn't even request it.

But, because I was so close to that group of students, I tried something I haven't done since. I had them write down all the hurtful things anyone has ever said or done to them. Then, with the aid of our maintenance director, we went outside to a burn barrel, with good old Pennsylvania snow falling on us, and walked up to the barrel and dropped the list into the fire inside the barrel.

Next, we went back inside and wrote down all the good that people had said about us and had done for us, and we kept those. It was a very powerful exercise, and I haven't had a group of kids that I felt would be as emotionally ready to try this type of healing technique since then, but it would be a very valuable tool to use if you felt you had a group who was mature enough to take it seriously to benefit from it.

This next presentation that I do with all my students every year is very powerful. Sometimes, your presentations can be curriculum-based and still be coaching classroom techniques meant to help them make positive decisions.

Even though I no longer teach freshmen, I still teach the contemporary novel I picked for my freshman students titled, *Sleeping Freshmen Never Lie* by David Lubar. I selected the book because I thought it had everything I was looking for in a novel to close the school year. It is an easy read by an author from Pennsylvania with a Pennsylvania setting so the students can relate to the references about snow days, hunting and fishing season, and so forth.

It is funny in that the main character, Scott, uses a great deal of satire and imagery to describe what is happening in the text. It deals with finding his way in school with old friendships he thought would last forever dissolving, navigating the emotions experienced with a crush, finding out his parents are going to have a baby, and also finding out that his older brother cannot read.

There is a traumatic part to that novel. It deals with an attempted suicide. An all-too-real problem with our youth.

I dislike saying, "fortunately" when I tell you about my next guest speaker, as I said previously about the other two, but as I stated, sometimes out of our greatest sorrows comes healing.

We had a teacher aide in our school whose son ended his life after his first seven days of college. She came to work with a smile on her face, and the kids absolutely loved her. So, when she comes into my classroom and tells them her story with tears streaming down her face, our students look at her as the pillar of strength and courage that she represents. What a blessing to have someone take something so tragic that happened to her and be able to use it to save our students.

We don't often know what people are going through when they walk through those doors every day. The most simplistic acts of kindness can make all the difference in the world.

Teachers are stationed at different places throughout our building each morning, each day of the week all year long, to help keep the students corralled in the cafeteria in the morning to wait for homeroom.

I noticed how mopey and tired students were as they meandered into the building. I started saying, "Good morning! Thank you for coming to school today!" At first, they would keep their heads down, not say anything in response, and try not to make eye contact. But I persisted.

I did it enough times that the other teacher assigned to the front door with me also began saying, "Good morning" to the students as they walked into the school. Many of them, though it took some time with quite a few, started to look at us, smile, and sometimes say, "Good morning" in return. Earbuds/Airpods have made greeting the students challenging, but not impossible.

It got to a point that if we were talking to someone when students came through the doors and we were going to miss addressing them, many of the students would say to us, "Good morning," or, "Hey, aren't you going to tell us good morning?" They missed hearing it.

Now, why did I start this trend? First of all, small wins lead to larger ones. Getting a kid who initially would not speak, make eye contact, or smile to do any or all three of these gestures is a great victory.

I also began this because I thought about the line from the novel *The Outsiders* by S.E. Hinton, in which Johnny says, "I think I like it better when the old man's hittin' me. At least then I know he knows who I am. I walk in that house, and nobody says anything. I stay away all night, and nobody notices."

While I realize that line is from a fictional text, it has always haunted me. A kid who would rather be hit than ignored. Think about some of our students' behavior issues and how they would rather get negative attention from us than none at all. Fictional text or not, you know that statement is true for so many of our students. Addressing them when they walk through the door lets them know we see them.

Everyone wants to be seen and heard. According to Psychology Today, "Being acknowledged by others helps you feel more accepted and secure." We all long to be validated. And, as Psychology Today also tells us, "Approbation from others whose authority we respect serves to verify our sense of inner worth. And such external approval is especially important for those still plagued with self-doubt."

Respect and self-worth. How do we get a society riddled with disrespect to respect us as educators, as figures in authority? I already addressed the issue of dealing with the negative public perception plaguing our careers as educators and how difficult it is to overcome. A once-noble profession now faces statements like, "Those who can't do, teach." Then you have the disrespect for authority figures in general. Our military, men and women in blue, and those in other leadership positions all have been the victims of mud-slinging. Are there authority figures who have made horrible mistakes, who are horrible people? Of course, but now those mistakes are helping to form a generalized public opinion of us that includes mistrust. Without trust, the disrespect follows. Vicious cycle.

However, we must rise above this unjust labeling and do our best to show students, parents, and community members that we are still a noble profession. I mentioned earlier that letting students know you care about them is a vitally important aspect of our jobs.

When they know you truly care, they will begin to trust you. When they trust you, you can then earn their respect. One of the ways you earn their trust is to treat them with respect.

Acknowledge their existence. Make your classroom a safe, welcoming place for them to go and learn. *The Coaching Classroom* techniques I provide for you to use, and then ideas you come up with on your own that fit your own unique teaching situation and students, will help show the students you care. When they believe you care, the mistrust and lack of respect typically go away. When students know we care and trust us, they then believe us when we recognize them, and their own feelings of self-doubt will dissipate, raising self-esteem. When a student feels better about himself/herself, the student will behave better and learn more.

Sometimes being real with them and sharing a few appropriate, not too personal, stories about our own lives helps them see us as imperfect humans like them instead of this no-worries authority figure. Seeing us in a different light can also help build trust between us and our students. Sometimes I will share a story with them about my life or just let them know how my day started. One morning I got in a fight with my husband, my dog got diarrhea, my kid mouthed off to me, my basement flooded, my car wouldn't start, and I had a killer sore throat. But I still came in and smiled and put forth my best efforts in my job.

When they hear the obstacles we face and overcome with a grin, they realize that power lies within them as well. Telling my students how my day started and then seeing me just carry on and do my job was me modeling a positive response to a lot of negativity. They listened intently. Some smiled. Some were shocked, but they mainly just listened and nodded with a look I deemed as appreciation for being forthright. Some wanted to play the "Oh, yeah? Well, listen to how much worse the start of my day was today, or *one time...*" game, but most just related silently. Using our own emotional intelligence, modeling what it looks like to be at our best when we have excellent reasons not to be, is a great way to get students to learn to disallow circumstances from controlling their actions and responses. And, they know that we are serious when we say that we can choose to be in a good mood or a bad one.

There was a time a few years ago that I couldn't help but come to work sad, and I wasn't sure what to do about it. You see, I loved my dog like a member of our family. She was an eleven-year-old little white West Highland Terrier. My husband let her out to go to the bathroom at the front of our house on the other side of our driveway, just as we had done for the past eleven years. He stepped away to get his cell phone charger and when he returned to the door, she was nowhere to be found (which was totally uncharacteristic of her). He decided to go outside to look for her, and when I realized what he was doing I quickly joined him. My daughter was home from college and joined us in our search. My son heard us yelling and woke up and came outside. My husband said something must have gotten her.

We live in a gated community in a wooded area, but we nor anyone in our community, to our knowledge, ever had an issue that would warrant concern about our pet being attacked. Something inside me made me dart for the woods at the back of the house after my husband made that statement. I found her immediately. She was still breathing but bleeding from a wound I could not see. Screaming and crying, I ran from the woods with her in my arms bleeding all over me. She died in my arms before we could try to save her.

I did not tell you this story to make you sad, especially if you are an animal lover like me. I simply wanted you to understand that having a pet die is difficult enough, but this incident was tragic and not a situation I could easily or quickly bounce back from the day after it happened.

So, how was I supposed to return to work knowing that the students would see how visibly shaken I still was about it? Worse yet, how could I repeat the story all day long without sobbing?

Since I knew they would realize there was something wrong with me and ask me about it, I decided to write down what happened on the board so that the students would understand. I did end it with the fact that I would eventually be okay, that I would never forget, but that I would be okay. I think that part of the message was important.

I still miss my dog and I still choke up thinking about how her life ended, but I am doing better. That too was important for students to see.

Now there is another reason I told you this story. I had a student in my first-period class who wrote down what I had put on the board. She wrote a message with it telling people to please reach out to me with a kind gesture, a story of their own, how they got through a tragedy of their own, and/or to write a note of sympathy.

The outpouring from my current students that year and students I no longer had in class was incredible. Did this young lady already have that kindness in her heart? I believe she did, but I also believe *The Coaching Classroom* inspired her to participate in this much-appreciated act of kindness. As I stated, once you change yourself and model those behaviors you desire, you will see changes in students as well.

CHAPTER 6

What About Outside of Work?

Ways to Teach and Increase Positivity
Beyond Your Classroom

The same practices we incorporate inside the classroom can be used outside of it with our family and friends. When I took a look at my own children, I was astonished at how hard I was working to incorporate positive practices in my classroom, but not everywhere else in my life.

The positivity jar is a great way to help our friends and family. When two friends of mine were diagnosed with cancer, I gave each of them a jar with positive quotes I had cut out for them. I mentioned earlier the film based on the book *The Secret* as having a lot of great information in it.

There is a clip from that book/film about a woman who is told she has cancer. She makes the decision to keep stress from her life as much as humanly possible and to repeat the mantra, "Thank you for my healing." Whatever she watched on the television was positive, humorous, and upbeat.

She knew how important it was for her to fill her life with positive language and laughter and stay away from stress. The positivity quotes I gave to my friends helped them stay positive during a very trying time in their lives.

Since the time that I gave those two friends the jars with positivity notes, I have had many friends and acquaintances receive a cancer diagnosis. I have made playlists of music with positive lyrics for them. I also bought them funny movies to watch. I have sent them uplifting text messages, emails, notes, and cards. I bought bracelets with inspirational messages on them. All of these efforts help people as they heal.

Joel Osteen talks about his mother being diagnosed with terminal cancer back in 1981. He says she hung up pictures all over her house that depicted her at a time when she was the epitome of health so that she had a visual of how she wanted to be once more. As of the time I am writing this book in 2020, she is still alive. The power of visualization backed by a burning desire is clear. Joel would also attribute her healing to the power of prayer and God's mercy.

Since visualization is so important, you could give people pictures of themselves healthy and having fun that they could look at to assist in their healing. Make a collage or copies of a bunch of photos of them with loved ones and friends doing what they love and help them hang them everywhere they look.

And, doing these kinds of acts does not just have to happen when people are sick with a physical ailment. I started a wellness group for staff at our school that would be based on random acts of kindness certificates, attendance, and work completed by the date requested. School personnel would put a certificate in the container in the mailroom with a statement about what the staff member did that was above and beyond the call of duty, and those statements were handed out to personnel at the monthly morning meetings. For every note the staff member received, a ticket was put in a container. Also, if the staff member did not miss a day of work that month, the staff member got another ticket put in the container.

Four tickets were drawn at the morning meeting by various staff members, and prizes were distributed to the winners. The first batch of prizes came to us from donations the wellness team members got for the initiative. The remainder of the prizes were supposed to come from our insurance company. They give us $1,000 a year for wellness initiatives. However, the insurance company didn't approve of any prizes that were for mental wellness because they claimed it had nothing to do with physical wellness. *What?*

I think most people have seen the commercial that says, "Depression hurts." In the commercial, a person is physically unable to take their dog for a walk or play with their kids when they are depressed because depression is a mental illness affecting their physical well-being.

While I am not in the medical field, I am convinced that mental and physical well-being go hand in hand based on what I have read and seen first-hand. Keeping yourself in a good mental state of mind can help you take care of yourself physically, so, wellness begins with the care of the mind.

The woman in *The Secret* clearly understood this connection, and as a result, her cancer disappeared without treatment. I am in no way suggesting that we go without proper medical attention if we become ill. I am also not suggesting that every ailment can be healed with our minds.

We are all going to get sick from time to time, and we are all going to die someday. However, I do believe that using our minds to help us stay well and get well faster does work. There is debate about this percentage, but I have heard many times before that we only use 10 percent of our minds.

While the movie *Limitless* was fiction, the idea of what we could accomplish if we could use more of our brains opened up the idea of what that might look like. For those of you unfamiliar with the film, Bradley Cooper takes a pill that allows him to use more of his mind, and what he accomplishes is incredible.

The movie *Split* was about an individual who was said to have twenty-four different personalities. The information was based on a real individual known as Billy Milligan. Billy had one personality that was right-handed, smoked cigarettes, played drums, another that painted portraits, another that played tenor sax and painted landscapes, another that was dyslexic, another that was deaf, another that played harmonica, and yet another that could speak in Serbian. How was that even possible? Some people believe that individuals with multiple personalities actually access more of their brains than the average person.

Either way, we cannot argue that the brain is the most powerful organ in our bodies. What we do with our mind, what we expose to it, is incredibly important. Exposing ourselves to more positive language and visuals often can only serve to strengthen us.

RULE #6

Keep positivity with you all day long, and you will become more positive, helping to influence those around you.

So, why not strengthen your own children's minds or the minds of other family members? I not only give positive-quote jars to friends battling illnesses; I have one on our pie safe in my kitchen.

We started out taking one a day, but as the habit of using the jar was formed, my husband and kids would pull a message out of it only when they needed or wanted it. Sometimes, when one of us begins to complain, I point at the jar, and the person doing all the complaining walks over and takes out a quote.

Reading the quote aloud and talking about it will often help the person change their focus from what was upsetting him/her to the message. Then, they seem to put in perspective the incident that was upsetting them.

I even went so far as using a hole punch on one end and attaching a piece of candy to the end of it using curling ribbon. These types of positivity quotes were used as a reward for doing something kind instead of just taking one when we elected to do so or when something was upsetting us.

Yes, I know some people will criticize me for using food, particularly candy, to reinforce positive behavior, and while we eat healthy in my household, I don't withhold sugar from my kids. I used M&Ms to potty train both of my children. Each trained at age two with no accidents with my daughter and only one accident with my son after only two weeks.

It did not cause them to overindulge in junk-food consumption. As a matter of fact, I ended up giving away the majority of their Halloween and Easter candy because they didn't eat it. So, I am sticking with my idea of candy on the positivity notes being an okay practice. The real point is that making positivity quotes available to your family is just as important as using it in the classroom.

We talked about gratitude earlier and how important it is to have an attitude of gratitude. Writing an old-fashioned thank-you note to people who have inspired you, who have been there for you, or made a difference in your life and sending it out to them is another way of incorporating positivity in your personal life which is infectious to those around you. Even if you don't want to mail a letter, you can call the person and say thank you or simply send a text. However, you chose to communicate it, showing gratitude toward others is good for the soul.

I believe that spirituality is also an important part of the journey toward a more positive life. This part of the book is not going to become a religious rant. Many people often confuse spirituality with religion. And, let's face it, religion is a touchy subject. If we define spirituality, according to Google, it means, "The quality of being concerned with the human spirit or soul as opposed to material or physical things."

Your spiritual journey is your own and personal. But spirituality is about seeking a meaningful connection with something bigger than yourself. Whether you find your spirituality through God or nature or art is totally up to you. I am in no way intending to influence or change your religious beliefs.

I just know, for me, that taking care of my soul through my faith is also a very positive part of my life. I have a book that my mother-in-law bought for us called *Jesus Calling*. The messages are short daily inspirational statements, and we read them in the morning during breakfast. This short time reading God's word is a good, positive start to our day.

We are all at different stages in our lives, and finding five minutes of peace and quiet may seem impossible for you right now. Just remember what I said about putting the oxygen mask on yourself first. To be the best person, teacher, spouse, friend, mother, father, child, and so forth that you can be, you must tend to your own needs first. If you truly want to make a change within, you will find a way.

For me, the hardest part of changing has been trying to avoid gossip. That includes listening to it and participating in it. I did not realize how so many people in my life, myself included, participated in it.

I used to try to tell myself it was okay because it was true, and it was okay to tell something if I knew for a fact it was the truth. But the fact remains that, true or false, it is not a positive practice.

Listening to and contributing to gossip is a negative practice. The issue is that even if it starts out innocently and is being used to help us assess our own lives, choices, and decisions, most gossip is malicious in nature and not told for any other purpose than to let others know the shortcomings of another individual or group of people. It is us passing judgment on others, and our judgments are only how we perceive a situation, not necessarily whether it is truly right or wrong.

And, is what we are discussing any of our business anyway? No, it is not. I cannot stress enough the importance of recognizing the negative impact gossip has on us and to walk away from it when our friends, family, or colleagues begin to gossip. Above all else, do not partake in it.

Again, it is never done in the spirit of positivity. It is done to cause harm to another person. Those kinds of situations cannot keep us in a positive frame of mind by subjecting ourselves to it or by adding to it.

We cannot grow personally or professionally when we entertain negativity. None of us is perfect, and we all will unfortunately fail to do what is right any number of our times in our lives, but as we practice making these changes in both our professional and personal lives, our negative choices should lessen. When we do make a negative choice, it is important to pick ourselves up, dust ourselves off, and try again. The fact that we recognized it and turned it around is the key to becoming the role model we wish to become for ourselves, our students, and our family and friends.

CHAPTER 7

Fresh Ideas for the Classroom

Creating a Unique Coaching Environment
that Best Fits You and Your Students

You are welcome to incorporate my ideas, but the fun part is coming up with new ideas and making your own coaching classroom climate that fits your personality and goals. After all, you know what feels natural for you and what will work for your students. But, don't feel bad if you try something and it doesn't work out the way you planned.

Arianna Huffington said, "We need to accept that we won't always make the right decisions. That we will screw up royally sometimes— understanding that failure is not the opposite of success; it's part of success." Doing what is safe in the classroom is not always doing what is best. Doing what is best will not always work out. It is no different than trying a new academic lesson and realizing that it was an epic failure. We have all had those kinds of lessons as well. Looked great when we came up with it and put it on paper, but the implementation of it was a whole other story. After all, teaching is a learning process for us as much as the students, and their success is our feedback.

So, in order to be successful, we have to be innovative. I have never used the same test in twenty-nine years of teaching. Even if it is similar, it is never the same because I teach the lesson differently each year.

I mean, if Krissy Gasbarre had written a book about transgenderism fifteen years ago, I doubt anyone would have read it. As a matter of fact, many would have chastised her for bridging the topic. Today, her book, *Raising Ryland*, has been embraced as an important work on a poignant topic. Just like our academic lessons, our coaching lessons must also be geared toward the group and what is happening currently in society.

RULE #7

You have never been teaching so long that you cannot implement change.

One of the ideas I will incorporate is a student of the month. We do a student of the month for the entire school presently, but I plan to do one for each class period. The criteria for being voted as student of the month will be created by the students along with me. The students will also help me determine the perks for being named student of the month. There will be an award that the student can retrieve from the front table each day and put on his/her desk to indicate that this student is the student of the month for that class. I will encourage the students to use criteria such as *kind, helpful,* and so forth. It is not an award for the student who does the best academically, but rather socially, giving a wider birth for more students to have the opportunity to receive it.

Remember what I said about the importance of acknowledgment? One year, our administration decided that we needed to have activity periods. With our school being a comprehensive vocational-technical school, there is little time in our schedule for anything except core content and career and technical education. Our only elective at that time was art, and every student was assigned to it at some point, like it or not. So, our administration, noticing that students had no downtime in their schedules, decided to let each instructor have a club of some kind that students could go to once a month. They shortened the other class periods and gave us an hour at the end of the day to implement these clubs once a week.

One year, I did an aerobic kickboxing club. Another year, I did a book club. One of the students who signed up for my book club was not really an avid reader, but he did attempt to do the assigned reading and participate in discussions with us.

During one of our reading sessions, we began discussing our own families and birthdays as they related to the information in the book we were reading. I mentioned a birthday party I was planning for my daughter. This senior male student, my non-avid reader of the group, told us that his mother left him when he was two years old. He said that not only had he never had a birthday party, he had never had a birthday cake.

I sat there in shock. I mean, we learn quickly as educators that not everyone lives the way we do, but this news broke my heart. As luck would have it, his birthday was only a few days after club time the following month. I had a cake all ready for him and made sure he arrived last to our meeting. We had the candles lit and sang "Happy Birthday." He cried like a baby…and so did the rest of us.

Something so simple and yet so important. I thought about that story as I was trying to come up with new ideas for my coaching classroom, and I have decided I will find out all of my students' birthdays and give them birthday cards. I will write inside, "I am so happy you were born and that you are in my class."

Another idea that has caught on around the world is gratitude rocks. No doubt you have been out somewhere and have seen rocks with positive messages etched in them. There are countless stories about people keeping special rocks in their pockets that remind them to be *Brave* or *Fearless* or *Strong*. I will work with our art department to create special rocks with positive messages that students can take with them.

Along the lines of using positive messages, I began looking for stickers I could use for student work. Unfortunately, the stickers I found were primarily for elementary education students. So, I took a bunch of positive phrases and had them printed as stickers. That way, I can put them on the top of student work and encourage them when they need it and celebrate successes as well.

This next idea would work better if I taught freshmen because students come to our school from four different school districts, but halfway through the year, I would like them to write down something nice about each classmate. I will put the list together and give them to each student.

I heard about a teacher who implemented this idea when I was listening to Joel Osteen. The positive messages the students received from their classmates were so powerful for them that when one of the classmates died in a war and the teacher and former classmates went to his funeral, they learned that he had the list in the pocket of his uniform when he died. After learning this fact about the list, the other classmates began to take their lists out as well. One carried it in his wallet, another in her purse.

What an impact something so simple had on these young people. They won't look back on their lessons on the different branches of government with fondness, but they will remember that lesson. While learning about such facets of the government is important, the most effective way to teach students is to make a positive lasting impression on them. Only then will we get true buy-in from the majority of our students.

We all have students who jump through the hoops we put in front of them because they recognize that they must excel academically to get into the college and pursue the career they desire. But what about the rest of our students who need to be convinced that learning is a positive endeavor? That is where our life lessons in *The Coaching Classroom* will enhance our academic lessons.

Each school year I evaluate the effectiveness of my coaching classroom concepts, just like I do with my academic instructional techniques. For example, the sticky notes may have been a success this past school year, but if students do not take them off the cabinet this upcoming school year, I may abandon that practice.

I may try it again the following year, but there again, I need to assess the group to see what practices are most useful in reaching them. Although reaching a large number of students is ideal, as I mentioned before, even if we reach one, we are making a difference.

It is important to review your ideas and look for new ones each school year. I realize that the more I get to know my students, the easier it is for me to come up with new ideas that might work in my coaching classroom.

CHAPTER 8

Why isn't Everyone as Excited I am Making These Changes?

How to Deal With the Naysayers and
Stay on Your Positive Path

As I stated before, you are obviously someone who went into education and stayed in education for all the right reasons if you are reading this book and are serious about making positive changes in your classroom. Yes, we are battling negative public perception, drug addiction, dysfunction in the homes, apathy toward learning, bureaucracy, and so much more. However, we can continue to use that as an excuse as to why real learning and connections in the classroom are not taking place, or we can do our part to make our classrooms the best they can be despite the obstacles we face.

We definitely have our work cut out for us. More and more people appear to prefer to complain and do nothing rather than do what it takes to reach today's youth. Unfortunately, some of your colleagues may fall into this category. The minute you begin to make positive changes in your classroom with coaching lessons and with academic lessons, you will be shocked to see how many of your colleagues will not be pleased with these changes.

Remember what I said about misery loving company? If you are busy doing something to bring about a positive change, that means you are no longer sitting around complaining about "these kids." Further, many will be afraid that the changes you make will be forced on them when the administration sees how well it is working for you in your classroom.

RULE #8

You decide what is best for you.

The fact of the matter is, you will have people in your life, whether it pertains to making positive changes in yourself or in the classroom, who will not support the changes you make. When I made these changes in myself, many of my friendships changed as well. The people I began to associate with changed.

Think about what released inmates, recovering alcoholics, and former drug addicts are all told when they complete their stint in jail or in rehab. The number one piece of advice those individuals are given is that they cannot go back to their old friends and frequented places or they will end up back where they started. There is a reason for that advice. Old habits die hard, and if you return to the negative people and places that got you into trouble in the first place, you will not stay out of trouble or stay clean.

That same principle applies to you. If you make positive changes in yourself and on the job but still surround yourself with negative family, friends, and colleagues, the chances of you being able to resist the temptation of sliding back into that negativity are next to zero.

Many people say that there is nothing we can do about negative family members. They are family, after all, and so we are stuck with them. While I don't suggest we stop speaking to our negative family members, I will suggest that we limit the amount of time we spend with them.

Just like watching the news. It is important to know what is happening in the world because living under a rock is not good either. However, we can gather enough information about the key events taking place around the world in about fifteen minutes of watching the news. We must limit our exposure to that negative information.

The same goes for family, friends, and colleagues for that matter. I have family members I love because they are family, but I don't necessarily like them, nor would I surround myself with them if we were not related. So, I am with them on a limited basis, and when I am in their presence, I work my mind very hard to try to keep the conversation positive. I really have to get my mind prepared to be with them beforehand. Being well-rested helps because I seem to be more open to suggestion and less cognizant of what is being discussed when I am tired.

With friends, the same thing happens. You can love certain friends from a distance. It does not matter that you have known that person since kindergarten. If the friendship is toxic for you, distance yourself. You don't have to tell the person that he/she is too negative and you are not going to hang out with them anymore. Just begin moving away slowly. He or she may get angry or hold on for dear life, but you need to do what is best for you.

Ironically, many people think that they owe family and friends and do not step away even when they find themselves stressed each time they encounter these individuals. I hear people say, "But she's my sister," or, "I have had this friend since I was five years old, and our parents are friends and our kids are friends."

It doesn't matter. The person you owe is yourself. You owe it to yourself to surround yourself with people who are uplifting and supportive. Love yourself enough, and value yourself enough to spend your precious time and energy on people who deserve it.

With colleagues, it can also be difficult. If you must be around those negative colleagues, you will have to get your mind in the right place to handle it. Get rested, meditate, use gratitude, limit the time if you can. Do whatever it takes to avoid being negatively impacted by those individuals. If you fail to keep positive and fall back into a pattern of complaint, don't give up. Start over. We all give in to those temptations. Recognize the behavior and turn it around.

I have found that if my life is not going well, if I am running into obstacle after obstacle, that is the universe's way of screaming at me to notice something that needs changed within. I stop and self-reflect for as long as I need to in order to figure out what I am doing to draw all this turmoil to me. It can be difficult to accept, but we are often our own worst enemy and bring about our trials and tribulations. The key is to see it and change it.

Now, I have come so far that if I am in a conversation with people who are more interested in complaining or being judgmental or gossiping, I actually feel bad in the pit of my stomach in their presence. Whenever possible, I find a way to step away from the conversation, or I do my best to turn the negative energy around.

I was most concerned about how our guidance department would take the coaching classroom techniques. It works one of two ways. The counselor either feels you have overstepped your bounds because you are responsible for teaching and the counselor is responsible for counseling. Or, the counselor recognizes that your contributions have nothing to do with you replacing what he or she does but that it makes the job a lot easier because you are teaching the students coping techniques so that the little issues the counselor was often inundated with before are often handled by the student. The counselor is only called in for the bigger issues.

The first guidance counselor we had in the building when I first started teaching was incredibly threatened when any student wanted to talk to a teacher instead of her. Since I was so much younger, I was more approachable than the counselor. This caused a major rift between her and me.

Our current counselors have welcomed the changes I have made in the classroom. They recognize the value in what I am doing and see that it helps them do their job more efficiently, and they have enough self-confidence to not feel threatened when students talk to other personnel.

If you are in a building with a guidance department that is like the counselor from my first years of teaching, be sure to include the counselors in what you are doing right from the beginning. This way, you will allow them to see that you are not trying to replace them. As long as you reinforce the concept that you're trying to support the counselors by teaching students coping skills, hopefully, the counselors will embrace what you are doing.

Since many have had training on the importance of building a student's self-worth, you may even opt to ask the counselors for some ideas you can implement in the classroom. Further, you could include the counselors in incorporating the ideas.

One of the challenges associated with *The Coaching Classroom* is that it can be misunderstood if we do not communicate what we are doing. There are some faculty and staff to whom you could explain the concept, and they would still find fault with what you are doing, but the resistance often occurs due to inadequate understanding. Like I said in the introduction, most will think you are overstepping your bounds, that your role in the classroom is to simply supply students with academic preparation, and that the parents, counselors, and other programs are in place to do the coaching. The key is to teach people that you are not replacing the role of anyone else. You are supplementing what they do with simple, positive practices.

Parents may also rebel against what you are doing. When I was having students write in their journals before I started vision boards, I had a mother complain that I was trying to make her son write a diary to tell me his feelings, and that was not my job. You have to decide how much you share with the parents about what you do. Do you tell them ahead of time or deal with concerns as they arise?

I let them know in my syllabus that we do a number of exercises to promote a positive attitude for a positive learning environment. I have had a few comments made by parents here and there, like the one mentioned above. However, most are very receptive.

Most parents have a difficult time arguing that doing something in the classroom that helps create a positive learning environment for their child is a bad idea. But, there are those few who will find fault, and they are usually the parents who take issue with everything the school does anyway. I give parents the general concept of what I am doing in the classroom and then deal with concerns as they arise.

For me, keeping my administration informed has been imperative. They are the ones who often get the phone calls from the few parents who want to find fault with any teacher who does something that varies from the norm. When my administration knows what I am doing and why, any concerns that arise are handled with complete support because they are well aware of what I do and why I do it. Again, if you collaborate with the counselors, you will have more credibility if a parent voices a concern, and it will make it even easier for administration to support your endeavors.

When we are faced with any kind of resistance, it can make us question the validity of what we are doing. Think about being in school and peer pressure. I am often very disappointed with anyone who only brings in guest speakers who have become alcoholics or drug addicts and gotten clean.

My mother has brought up this point, and it has become my stance on the matter as well. While it is important for people to see that a person who becomes an addict can turn his/her life around, why don't we ever promote the person who resisted becoming an alcoholic and drug addict to teach people how to avoid becoming an addict? Those people are equally important to listen to because they help us take preventative measures to avoid having the problem in the first place.

I mean, it had to be incredibly difficult not to drink and use drugs when so many people around them were using, especially if these people were popular in school and still managed to resist it and remain popular. Most get shunned if they don't follow the crowd. Why? Because it is difficult to do what is right.

The same goes for trying something new in the classroom. Did you ever hear that saying, "It is lonely at the top?" It's true. Sometimes doing the right thing, doing what you know is best for you and your students, can leave you feeling lonely. There were times I have been so excited to share my personal and professional successes with people I thought for sure would be happy for and celebrate with me. I have been astonished at their reactions.

Many have let me down by giving me a negative response. That response from a person I value made it even more difficult to continue doing what I am doing. It made me question myself. Then, you have the student who resists what you are doing and gives you a bad time. Then. a colleague gets on your case for all the time you waste doing "silly" little lessons when you should be teaching your core content. Your "friend" says you are no fun anymore. All these unfavorable responses may leave you questioning the changes you are making. That feeling is totally understandable. Just remember what I discussed previously about everything that is worthwhile taking more effort and being more challenging.

Also, please recall what I mentioned about people who were challenged and gave up. Don't walk away when you are three feet from gold. Hang in there and do what is best. Eventually, these people will get on board with you or they will steer clear. If they walk away, they have done you a favor.

Remember the saying, "We should constantly evaluate our relationships. Every person who is in our lives now is not always supposed to be in our life forever. If you don't get rid of the wrong people, you will never make room for the right people to come into your life." Make room for the right people and the right experiences. I promise you that it is worth it.

The friendships I have now are with wonderful, real, positive people. Listening to my kids come up with peaceful resolutions to problems that arise in our household or with their friends is also rewarding. I found colleagues who genuinely care about student success that I can collaborate with on instruction. My marriage is stronger. And, I am reaching students. It is all because I made a change, stuck with it, tried again when I faltered, and trusted myself.

CHAPTER 9

The Proof is in the Pudding

Data and Statistics that Back up
The Coaching Classroom and its Techniques

I said it was working. I am reaching students. How do I know for sure? How can I be certain I am making a difference by creating a coaching classroom? Don't just take my word for it. The data and testimonials prove the value of *The Coaching Classroom*.

Most people in education know that there are innumerable ways of looking at data and a plethora of sites that offer to analyze it for us. The information I am providing here is from the information sent to us from the state based on our student testing. If you look at the aggregated data available on our test scores, you will see that the numbers vary slightly, but in each case, the test scores went up for students from my class who took the Keystone Literature exam when I began implementing coaching classroom techniques.

It is not that I am teaching how to analyze the significance of the theme in a text that much better than I did years ago. I am teaching the students to do their best. I am helping the students believe that they can be proficient on these exams. I am incorporating life coaching into the classroom, and it is helping emotionally as well as academically.

According to the Perkin's Data, retrieved for me from our school director, Dr. Barry Fillman, over a three-year period (2014 to 2017), with me being the only teacher teaching the students who tested and after incorporating life coaching techniques in the classroom, test scores for the Keystone Literature exams went from 29.7 percent to 57.14 percent. That is a 27.44 percent increase over a three-year period. It is also noteworthy to mention that, during that time, all students from all ability levels were transitioned into my classroom, resulting in full academic inclusion. During 2018 and 2019, I was no longer the only instructor teaching sophomores and our test scores leveled out, with variations in a couple of percentage points here and there. In the spring of 2020, we obviously did not test.

These test scores are getting the attention of people outside our school. As part of ESSA (the Every Student Succeeds Act, signed into existence on December 10th, 2015, by then-President Barack Obama), schools are expected to begin to create a plan to assist in improving the total student.

Our administration decided to put together a group of our faculty members to help create a more positive environment for our students. As stated above, one of the goals of ESSA is to put efforts in place to improve the total student.

Our administration used a term from their training to name the team PBIS, which quite simply stands for Positive Behavior Interventions Support. In an effort to see what other schools like us in our region are doing to improve, our group recently traveled to the Lawrence County Career and Technical Education Center in New Castle, Pennsylvania. While we were at the school, the school officials asked my principal, Mrs. Melissa Mowrey, what we were doing to get our test scores to increase so dramatically.

There are eighteen comprehensive vocational-technical schools in the state of Pennsylvania. In 2012, our school was ranked seventeenth out of eighteen schools on our Keystone test results. Between 2013 and

2017, we moved from seventeenth to sixth in the state in Keystone test scores. As of 2020, there are sixteen comprehensive vocational-technical schools in the state of Pennsylvania.

My coaching classroom techniques are not the only reason for such a jump in our test scores. New administration, a change in instructors who teach the core content to the students being tested, and some innovative practices have also impacted our overall performance. But in English, where I was the only sophomore instructor when our test scores rose so dramatically, I attribute *The Coaching Classroom* techniques to the increase in the literature scores.

If simply creating a coaching classroom to improve the well-being of your students is not enough to convince you and your administration to adopt these practices, using these techniques, along with the use of other instructional strategies, can help you meet the requirements of ESSA and improve your school's standardized test scores.

Further, if you are coming from a school in Pennsylvania, *The Coaching Classroom* techniques can help you and your school meet the goals outlined in the state-wide PBIS (Positive Behavior Intervention and Support) initiative, often known as the School-Wide Positive Support Behavior or SWPSB. It is a team-based process that, according to my school principal, Melissa Mowrey, focuses on being "proactive in teaching, monitoring, and supporting school-appropriate behavior for all students." The goal is to recognize and reward student strengths in favor of concentration on their weaknesses. This is a research-based program that attempts to ward off negative behaviors in creating a positive learning environment. The techniques I have used in my classroom will dovetail well with the mission of this initiative.

ESSA has begun to require schools to move toward positivity, and our PBIS team has employed some of the ideas I used in *The Coaching Classroom*, as well as come up with some fantastic ideas of their own. In response to this focus, our school began by having the girls' restrooms painted in bright colors with positive quotes painted on the walls—

much like my classroom. Through PBIS, a student organization was also formed, and they named themselves Aevidum, which means, "I've got your back." This group is coming up with ideas to spread positivity throughout the school.

Need more proof that I am making a difference using *The Coaching Classroom* techniques? I received positive feedback that the coaching classroom is working. I had a student who did not pass her Keystone Literature exam. She was placed in my remediation class to help prepare her to retake the exam in the winter. I worked with her on the content, but I spent more time teaching her that she could in fact pass this test.

She later told me that she earned the highest score out of all the students who had to retake the exam in December. A score of 1500 is passing, and hers was 1591. She credited me with helping her achieve success on the exam and said,

> "Mrs. Mulhollan had an extremely big impact on me. Not only did she teach me what I needed to pass a very important test, but she gave me the confidence I needed to get the highest score. I had very little confidence. When I was three, my family was told I had autism. And, in addition to this diagnosis, they were told I had learning disabilities as well. All through elementary school and middle school, people had very low expectations of me. Mrs. Mulhollan expects each student to work hard and do his/her best. Because she treated me the same as all her other students, and didn't take, 'No, I can't do it,' for an answer, I felt like I could do it. She believed in me, and that made all the difference." –Ande G.

Another example of feedback that I received that let me know *The Coaching Classroom* is working is receiving the Teacher of the Year award in 2016. With our new administration, my principal and director started a Teacher of the Year contest. This contest had only been in place for two years when I won during the third year of its inception.

Students nominate teachers, and then a winner is chosen. As I stated before, my school has Career and Technical Educational training. Those instructors have their students their freshman through their senior years, so they become very close to those instructors.

Just to give you an example of how close our students become to their Career and Technical instructors, one of our students asked his CTE instructor to be his emergency contact person on his personal information.

The first year of the contest, our Cosmetology CTE instructor won, and the second year our Culinary CTE instructor won. The third year, I was astounded when my name was announced as Teacher of the Year. My classroom requirements were more challenging than they have been in all the years I had been teaching, and yet I still won. I was honored beyond belief. Students nominate a teacher, and then a teacher is selected from those nominations. I would like to share what the student who nominated me wrote.

"Mrs. Mulhollan is a kind-hearted teacher who actually cares. She gives you advice on everything that you throw at her. She is unlike any teacher I know. She not only teaches you lessons, but also makes sure you know the objectives she is teaching. She will even reword it 1,000 times, if need be, to make sure you understand. Mrs. Mulhollan will give you positivity quotes, validate you, and even have you do things she knows are good for you. She is like an English Mom, and I thank her a lot for everything she has done for me. I personally believe that she should not only be teacher of the year, but the greatest teacher of this country." –Kayla B.

I had so many students congratulate me for my Teacher of the Year award, and at the end of the school year, so many students thanked me for everything I taught them. Here is part of one letter I received at the end of that school year.

"There have been many days where I felt down or alone, and your kind words, and positive attitude, lifted my spirit. You helped me realize that I'm worth more than I thought I was and I can make something of myself and be the best me I can be." She also said, "Every word of encouragement, every positive quote, every story and speech has given me a new positive view on everything I encounter. You're such a wonderful teacher." -Anna Bea M.

I have a learning support teacher who is scheduled in my classroom with me when I have learning support students. I typically have one to two classes with learning support students each day. The learning support instructor, Ms. Diane Oberlin, who had been assigned to my classroom to support these students, saw first-hand the impact *The Coaching Classroom* had. She stated,

"I am a learning support instructor who has been scheduled with Mrs. Mulhollan for the past ten years. I supported her sophomore English class both before and after she began incorporating life coaching techniques into it. I have seen a number of changes in the way Mrs. Mulhollan instructs her classes. It was always evident that she cared about her students' well-being and success. However, with the use of life coaching, she has discovered a better way of showing it and has given students skills they can use to help them both in and out of school and for the rest of their lives.

I began my career working at a mental health facility for six years. I have now been in education for the past twenty-nine years. I have watched students struggle with the stress of dealing with such issues as family problems, friendship and other relationship issues, grades, social media, and peer pressure associated with the use of drugs and/or alcohol. Mrs. Mulhollan has always looked for ways to improve her teaching. I don't think she has ever done the exact same thing from year to year. Now, she uses life coaching in her classroom and even makes changes to that each year as well.

One of the most profound effects I have seen life coaching do for our students is to give them a feeling of hope. When she is giving them positive reinforcement through the discussions she has with them, I have watched them intently focus on every word she is saying. You can literally see how the conversation lifts the burden off many of their shoulders and helps them find self-esteem they may have lost somewhere along the way. Mrs. Mulhollan has asked students to set goals for themselves, which has allowed them to work toward achieving what they want out of life. By focusing on what they want, and what they can do, many students are seeing a way out of unfavorable living situations.

From the quotes to the stories to goal setting to the vision boards, and so much more, these activities have provided our students with so much more than simply giving them the best way to pass a standardized test or dissect a poem. After all, the life lessons we give to our students are the ones that truly help them learn everything else."

Administrative support makes creating a coaching classroom much easier. When you have administrators who allow you to try new ideas to reach students, who encourage you to try something new to help students not only do well academically but to get students to be more successful as individuals, you can make the most of creating a coaching classroom. My administration not only supported my endeavor to incorporate life coaching techniques in my English classroom but because of the success of it, my principal and school director allowed me to write a curriculum to create a coaching classroom stand-alone course that I called Foundations for Life. The course is a half-year humanities credit class for all incoming freshmen. There are three units for the course, which include Success/Professionalism, Career Readiness, and Self-Care. I am fortunate to have administrators who put students first and who support my classroom. My director, Dr. Barry Fillman, had this to say about me and what I do in my classroom:

"I am glad that Melissa Mulhollan has decided to share her story. Having witnessed firsthand the impact of Melissa on students, I am grateful she is part of the mission at Jeff Tech. Walking into her classroom, you will see positive quotes on the wall, uplifting notes for students to take with them, and positive messages relayed in an effort to have students internalize her culture of belief and caring. The high standards she sets for students are supported by building positive relationships as a trusted mentor. I have no doubt the visualization of success that she leads students through positively impacts them as they focus on what they want to become and their own abilities that will help them get there.

Melissa mirrors the expectations she has for students by constantly striving to improve, taking on new opportunities and being an advocate for and leader of her peers. Her actions supporting the many new initiatives at Jeff Tech speak just as loudly as her words to those who know her. A true growth mindset is evident in how she approaches her craft. Students and colleagues alike know that Melissa truly sees them and values them. This gets the best out of those around her."

Between the increases in test scores, the positive feedback, and the support from administration, I know that *The Coaching Classroom* is helping me do the job I have been entrusted to do.

Seeing the success from incorporating *The Coaching Classroom* techniques allows us to discard old ideals that no longer work. The idea of not smiling before Christmas is definitely no longer good teaching advice. While I know that is not literal advice and simply means to be strict initially so that you do not lose control of your classroom, I think it is important to know that you can be a caring and kind instructor and still be a classroom management guru.

Why do we need these coaching techniques in the classroom? Beyond what we all see in our profession, Peggy Caruso, executive and personal development coach, author, eight-time entrepreneur, and my mentor and friend, coaches students and has seen first-hand the need for schools to incorporate these techniques. She says,

"Being a successful executive and personal development coach, I am of the opinion that incorporating coaching into the educational system would serve as an asset. I deal with many children, teens, adults, and family situations, therefore allowing me to experience positive and negative behavioral patterns. Coaching is a very effective model that creates positive behavioral changes and recognizes saboteurs, while simultaneously strengthening our greater inner core.

Professionally speaking, everyone needs to continually strive to implement positivity and recognize negative patterns that need to be changed. I feel it is essential to incorporate the coaching into the educational system because my experience with the children/teens exemplifies how education, combined with family values and coaching techniques, creates an awareness to recognize what needs to be changed.

Recognizing the awareness assists with creating a strategic plan of action to replace the negativity with positivity, implement the goals, and establish the inner core strengthening to provide the solution.

As a professional coach, I have personally experienced how those positive behavioral changes have incorporated new coping methods in the classroom. Some examples of the behavioral issues I deal with involve communication, bullying, increasing grades, creating new study habits, depression, ADD/ADHD, family issues, fears, etc. Applying coaching techniques in the classroom enhances the educational process.

Being an eight-time entrepreneur, I have implemented success principles in the children I have coached. It has been very successful. Teaching success principles helps to redirect negativity in the child, and it creates the desire to set and reach goals. Instilling goal-setting in children at a young age helps to stimulate positive behavior as they mature. Many parents will make the statement that their child may not desire the entrepreneurial realm as they enter adulthood. They do not have to become an entrepreneur, but learning success principles will assist them as they venture into the corporate arena.

Success principles go hand-in-hand with leadership training. Whether it is within a corporate setting or classroom, leadership training paves the way for understanding the importance of leading and/or following and how strengths and weaknesses affect performance.

So, how do success principles relate to the implementation of coaching in the educational system? Implementing success principles assists with the basic fundamentals in education. It provides them with the four Cs (collaboration, creativity, communication, and critical thinking), which we are all familiar with. Coaching assists with expansion on the four Cs by incorporating family values. In essence, the child/teen utilizes that combination within the classroom setting, as well as creating new friendships. The positive mindset along with new tools/techniques links learning across subjects and disciplines. This new behavior brings harmony within the educational system.

Teaching children and teens to focus on positive change assists with eliminating bullying, low self-esteem issues, cutting, etc. Nothing bad can come from positive reinforcements. Children who bully others have somehow allowed negative influences to dominate their personality, and coaching assists with recognizing where the negativity came from and providing tools and techniques to change it.

Implementing coaching in the classroom can only create positive change and techniques to strengthen that change. It would assist with the creation of positivity into adulthood. Coaching creates balance and helps to enhance self-esteem in the child/teen. It teaches gratitude, effective communication, and mindfulness. Once a child learns to be grateful and mindful of their own inner self, it will then create a sense of respect to others."

How many times did you hear someone famous bring up a time when a teacher inspired or humiliated them? On more than a dozen occasions, I have seen famous people on TV mention something teachers said to them. It stuck with them all through their lives, so much so that they mention it as a moment that resulted in their success, or they are bringing it up to show the teacher that they made it in spite of their criticism. What we do and say matters. We need to remember that fact, no matter how "these kids" come to us.

There have been times when I have gone to my family doctor for an issue and he has had to refer me to a specialist. We are not a failure if we work to help a student who needs more help than we can offer.

I had a student one year who would have a few little successes, but so many more setbacks. I had to remove her more often than not because she would take away from the educational rights of others. I do not consider her my failure. There is so much more this student needed than a coaching classroom could provide to her.

Just like a family physician, I recognized that she needed more intense assistance than the simple classroom techniques I was employing. I didn't give up on her. I just directed her to people who might be able to help her and kept her from infringing on the educational rights of my other students.

Some of you might be saying, "Must be nice. My whole class acts like that and I cannot send them off for help." I get that we are all coming from totally different situations, and I am not suggesting that what works for me is the cure-all for you. I can promise you that caring for your students, getting them to see that you care, and helping them to value themselves using these life coaching techniques will work with most of your students, no matter how pristine or difficult your teaching job may be.

I acknowledged earlier that though some students are resistant to the positivity I use in the classroom, I have had success. I wanted you to see that the students I have reached have made it all worthwhile. The successes have outweighed any issues I may still have with some other students. After all, if we are the only ones incorporating these practices in our classrooms, we may not have enough time to break through the barriers some students have put in place.

The change is gradual and may move more slowly than we would like, but it is happening. It is best to have the techniques of *The Coaching Classroom* working throughout the school, but we can make a change in the climate even if we are the only ones striving to make that change. After all, in the words of Oskar Schindler, "Whoever saves one life, saves the world."

Recommended Reading

100 Ways to Enhance Self-Concept in the Classroom by Jack Canfield

Feng Shui Your Life by Jayme Barnett

Help Yourself by Dave Pelzer

Make the Impossible Possible by Bill Strickland

Strength in Stillness by Bob Roth

The Power of Habit by Charles Duhigg

The Secret by Rhonda Byrne

The Sleep Revolution by Arianna Huffington

Think and Grow Rich by Napoleon Hill

About the Author

MELISSA MULHOLLAN has been an educator for nearly 30 years. She became a certified life coach in 2014. She wrote her new book, *The Coaching Classroom,* to share life coaching strategies she has used to help her students improve their performance and reach their full potential.

This initiative was so successful that Melissa now teaches a stand-alone course using the coaching techniques she discusses in her book, along with other success principles. The course is called Foundations for Life and focuses on three units: Success and Professionalism, Career Readiness and Self-Care.

Melissa has been a member of the school's building leadership team since its inception in 2015 and was voted Teacher of the Year in 2016. She has served in her local teachers' union as secretary for two years, vice president for eight years and president for the past three years.

Her passion for the well-being of children extends beyond her classroom. Melissa is donating 10% of the proceeds of her book to ImPACT Virginia, a 503(c)3 nonprofit organization dedicated to educating medical students and the healthcare community to understand human trafficking as a growing public health issue. In partnership with the VCU School of Medicine in Richmond, Virginia, ImPACT Virginia created a curriculum on human trafficking which they plan to share, free of charge, with other medical schools across the country. Every year, ImPACT Virginia partners with 4th-year medical students at VCU and UVA Schools of Medicine, to host a free multi-day Medical Symposium on Human Trafficking which draws prominent local and national experts in the field. They will soon be launching a free 6-week support group for the family and friends of survivors of human trafficking. Melissa's donation will go toward the development and implementation of these programs. Melissa, along with English Instructor, Lyndsey Tamburlin, will be assisting ImPACT in the development of the curriculum for the courses.

Melissa resides in DuBois, PA with her husband and son.

To learn more about Melissa, *The Coaching Classroom,* and the Foundations for Life curriculum, please visit www.melissamulhollan. com.